The Worth of a Woman's Words

Selected Titles by Dianna Booher

Fresh-Cut Flowers for a Friend

Love Notes

First Thing Monday Morning

Ten Smart Moves for Women Who Want to Succeed in Love and Life

Communicate with Confidence!

Get a Life Without Sacrificing Your Career

Get Ahead, Stay Ahead

Clean Up Your Act!

Great Personal Letters for Busy People

The Letterwriter's Almanac

To the Letter

Winning Sales Letters

The Executive's Portfolio of Model Speeches

67 Presentation Secrets to Wow Any Audience

To-the-Point E-mail and Voice Mail

Would You Put That in Writing?

Writing for Technical Professionals

Good Grief, Good Grammar

Cutting Paperwork in the Corporate Culture

Send Me a Memo

The New Secretary

People Power

The Worth
of a
Woman's Words

THE POWER OF WHAT WE SAY
TO BUILD OR DESTROY, HEAL OR HURT,
INSPIRE OR DISCOURAGE

Dianna Booher

WORD PUBLISHING
NASHVILLE
A Thomas Nelson Company

Published by Word Publishing, Nashville, Tennessee

ISBN: 0-8499-3735-3

Printed in the United States of America
99 00 01 02 03 04 05 06 QPV 9 8 7 6 5 4 3 2 1

Contents

Acknowledgments ix
May I Have a Word with You? xi

Words that

Protect: Time Doesn't Heal All Wounds 1
Promise: Are You Out for Good, or Just on Furlough? 7
Delay: I've Been Meaning to Do That. 11
Prove: A Long, Long Walk. 14
Cheer: Who Wants to Be *Normal?* 16
Praise: Picking Eggs 19
Determine: Earn It or Steal It 23
Model: Playing Ping-Pong Sober 25
Love: Who Said I Didn't Notice? 29
Challenge: Don't Be What I Want You to Be 31
Gossip: It's True—Just Go Ask Your Mother 34
Motivate: First Thing Monday Morning 38
Judge: Can You Imagine That?. 45
Mold: Work Ethic or Worry Ethic? 48
Dispel Fear: Oreo Cake and Amazing Grace 51
Enlighten: Daughters of Privilege 57
Punish: From Dusk to Death 60

Sabotage: Amy, Nancy, Cindy, Courtney, Whoever 63

Pray: The Wide-Eyed Son. 67

Forgive: The Girl in Green 70

Lie: More or Less. 75

Disappoint: Math Mountains. 80

Comfort: Going Home 83

Label: Do You Know Joe? 86

Inspire: Go, Girl 89

Accept: I'd Like You to Meet My Wife. 92

Question: The Rules in Our House 96

Scold: Now Look What You Did! 100

Uplift: Where Did I Go Wrong?. 103

Laugh: All the Way to the Tub 106

Manipulate: Kids Nowadays 108

Trouble: Did You Notice Your Arm?. 111

Reject: With Friends Like These 115

Discourage: Sure You Can't 119

Understand: Before You Say "I Do". 122

Warn: Not My Brother, He Isn't 125

Remember: Rings, Beaus, and Horses. 130

Limit: So Trill Your R's 132

Affirm: Life in the Middle Lane. 135

Accuse: Interviews and Inquisitions 138

Advise: How to Meet a Man. 143

Bridge: To Russia with Love 147

Calm: I Never Got the Call!. 151

Support: Passion and Plans. 154

Blame: A Strong Will and Stricken Heart. 157

Trust: Don't Leave Home Without It 160

Clarify: Why Celebrate Tuesdays? 162

Dare: Stand Up, Speak Up, Move On. 167

Compliment: Diets and Dreams. 170

Criticize: Now You Do, Now You Don't. 172

Cast Doubt: Any More Encouraging Thoughts? 177

Encourage: When I Grow Up 179

Divide: Mirror, Mirror, on the Wall 183

Embarrass: Mars, Not the Moon 187

Free: I'm Home! 191

Discern: Will Work for Food. 195

Hover: Name That Tune 199

Defend: Not the Katlin I Know 201

Haunt: Where the Resemblance Ends. 203

Needle: Tennis Not-Tos. 206

Teach: Yell Politely 209

Nudge: Quips and Quotes, Not "Quit" 212

Rattle: If You're So Smart, Why Ain't You Rich? 214

Thank: No Fingers but a Grateful Heart 217

Tease: Payday 221

Warm: Four Husbands and a Veil 223

Trap: Hold the Cheese. 226

Heal: For the Sake of Sisters 229

Admire: I've Become My Mother 232

The Final Word 234

For More Information 236

Acknowledgments

A great big thank-you to the many people who thoughtfully answered my ubiquitous questions during the last few months: "Do you recall high-impact words and conversations with an important woman in your life—a spouse, mother, grandmother, daughter, sister, aunt, friend, teacher, or coworker? What made a positive or negative impact on you? What marked a turning point in a relationship? Set a plan in motion? Gave you new insight, hope, or faith?"

With those questions, many funny, sad, frightening, and inspiring stories—and sometimes tears—surfaced.

Specifically, I want to thank the following people for sharing their conversations and memories that led to this book: Opal Daniels, Sandy Daniels, Leanne Daniels, Keith Daniels, Angie Casey, Lisa McGown, Jeff Booher, Jennifer DeBorde, Mark Nettles, Karen Rinehart, Jenivie Isgitt, Andrea Haase, Suzanne Brimmer, Diana Ramsey, Valerie Sokolosky, Stephanie Sokolosky, Lynne Ritchie, Lynelle Goff Eddins, Katherine Durbin, Kim Collins, Bill Collins, Tracey Nosko, Dottie Walters, Lilly Walters, Maggie Bedrosian, Nancy Koenig, Darla Duscay, Beth Clark, Mary Lou Fehr, Polly Fuhrman, Rachel Lane, Vicky Ulrich, Jim Ramsbottom,

Vernon Rae, Marguerite Herd, Juanita Dunn, Sherry Clay, CJ Seaman, Wanda Richerson, Charles Thornton, Ken Reimer, Jann Mitchell, Gloria Pearson, and many other people who will remain nameless because I questioned them in taxis, airports, and speech audiences!

Thanks to each of you. And my heartfelt appreciation to Lee Gessner, editor-in-chief, and all the other staff at Word Publishing who caught the vision about the power words wield in our lives. We can change the world with words.

May I Have a Word with You?

I've lost more sleep over words than from any illness, work, or obligation in my life. Words that I wish I'd said and didn't. Words that I've said and wished I hadn't. Words that others have said to me that cut deep. Words that others didn't say to me that still managed to leave a hole in my psyche. Words that rolled off my tongue too quickly. Words that I swallowed and held onto too long.

Words can change our lives forever. Women have overcome seemingly insurmountable obstacles with the insight offered by a friend's advice. With words, the sick have gained courage to live. With words, friends have bonded for life. With words, husband and wife have become one. With words, teachers have inspired underachievers to become leaders. With words, leaders have motivated peasants to change the world. With words, citizens have overthrown tyrannical governments and changed the course of history.

Let me get more specific. With our positive words, we can accept, admire, admit, advise, affirm, apologize, ask, bridge, build, calm, challenge, cheer, clarify, comfort, compliment, confess, counsel, defend, determine, discern, discover, dispel fear, encourage, enlighten, evaluate, explain, extend, forgive, free, heal, include, inspire, introduce, laugh, lead, love, model, mold, motivate, nourish, persuade, plan, praise, pray, predict, prepare, promise, protect, prove, question, remember, reveal, seek, soothe, support, teach, tease, thank, trust, understand, uplift, warm, warn, welcome, and witness.

But, unfortunately, there are also negative words. With our negative words, we alarm, blackmail, blame, cajole, cast doubt, complain, confuse, contradict, cripple, criticize, dare, deceive, delay, diminish, disappoint, discourage, disillusion, distance, divide, embarrass, embellish, exclude, flatter, frighten, gossip, gripe, haunt, hover, insult, judge, label, lie, limit, manipulate, mislead, mock, needle, paralyze, punish, rattle, reject, sabotage, scold, stereotype, tattle, trap, and trouble.

Because of negative words, strong men have wept over their mothers' disappointment, uttered in anger. Because of words, marriages have ended in divorce. Because of words, grandmothers have lost contact with their grandchildren forever. Because of words, teens have committed suicide. Because of words, sisters haven't spoken to each other in years. Because of words, businesses have gone bankrupt. Because of words, leaders have fallen. Because of words, wars have killed millions.

In these pages I've focused on ordinary people—not poets, princesses, or presidents—for a purpose. Why? Because most of us won't be talking to heads of state. We talk to the people next door, to our brothers-in-law, to jealous coworkers, to teens with acne. The sum total of our life's relationships rests on our day in and day out interactions. Not the big events, but the simple conversations.

For the past few months, I've asked almost everyone I've spent more than a couple of hours with (and some I've spent only a few minutes with!) if they could recall a high-impact conversation with a woman. Most everyone could recall a certain conversation with a grandmother, mother, daughter, wife, aunt, cousin, coworker, or customer that had a significant impact on them—on their self-esteem, their plans, their principles, their values, their attitudes, their outlook, or their failures and successes in life.

They remembered. Common conversations can be profound.

That, in a nutshell, is my point: People remember words. Words have power—power to hurt or to help.

Most of us won't have opportunity to prevent great wars through an apt word spoken to a president or prime minister. We may not see our children grow up to lead a nation or feed the world's poor. But nearly all of us, with our words, will have a chance to influence those with whom we eat, play, shop, travel, work, and worship.

And the wonderful thing about words is that they're not fattening, expensive, or scarce! We don't have to be young or old to use them. We don't have to be healthy to say them. We don't even have to be particularly smart to spit them out. Everybody has access to this tool of influence.

It's my hope that through these pages containing tidbits of conversation and tales of emotion, you'll realize the anguish caused by careless words and the power of positive words to change lives.

There are few greater responsibilities in life than to weigh our words with wisdom and kindness. I'm listening. How about you?

Dianna Booher

❧ ❧ ❧

The bitterest tears shed over graves are for words left unsaid and deeds left undone.

—*Harriet Beecher Stowe*

Words that Protect

TIME DOESN'T HEAL ALL WOUNDS

Mrs. McGowen headed up the program committee for our school's annual Parents' Night. Every homeroom had to perform for the event: a chorus, a puppet show, a recitation of the Gettysburg Address, or a reenactment of the Pilgrims' first Thanksgiving feast. My fourth-grade class was assigned the square-dance number. Six couples were chosen to practice and perform. And practice, we did. Four weeks before curtain night, our teachers had us rehearsing during homeroom. Three weeks to the performance, practice became part of PE. Two weeks before the performance, practice cut our lunch periods short.

The week of the big event, we skipped writing, geography, and art classes in favor of all-out, dead-serious rehearsals. Our teacher's image rested on how well we do-si-doed; after all, how else could our parents know their kids were gaining an appreciation for art, music, and the finer things in life? Each of the six prepubescent boys had, in turn, received at least one paddling for "horsing around" during rehearsals. In the end, we were ready, with every clap, swirl, and step together.

But the crowd of parents seated in the bleachers above us sobered our thoughts the night of the performance. There was not a smile among us as we lined up, male and female, hand in hand. Animals parading into Noah's Ark couldn't have been any more somber about the occasion.

Last in a long lineup of acts to take the stage—the big circle painted in the center of the basketball court—we girls swirled our ruffled square-dance skirts as the petticoats swished with each step. In place beside us, the boys, wearing their western shirts with metallic buttons, stood frozen like cowboys ready for the first calf out of the rodeo chute.

Somebody backstage put the phonograph needle on the record, and we started the first promenade. Then about eight bars into "Skip to My Lou, My Darling," the needle skipped to another groove. The promenade music gave away to a different beat. Marvin grabbed my hand and pulled me into the center of the circle. Just about the time we figured out what to do next and started a new square-dance pattern, the needle jumped another groove.

Our eyes grew wider as we searched each others' faces for a clue on what move to do next. This time, Billy Ray took the lead, and we formed a big circle and skipped to the left. The needle jumped another groove, and Judy reversed the direction, yanking us to the right.

As the first and third couples swung their partners, Sue groped for hands and bunched us toward the small inner circle, whispering loudly over the garbled music, "No, no, it's promenade; it's promenade again." Who was going to argue with her? At least it was a direction. Half of us swirled; the other half skipped.

It was not at all like practice. All of a sudden, something felt loose around my hips. My sash? But there was no time to think about that; Marvin yanked me in the opposite direction again, and we started to promenade to the left. With the next jerk, my fears were confirmed.

My panties hung midthigh. Maybe if my do-si-do steps were high enough, I could work them back up. How many more grooves could the record possibly have? Why didn't our teacher have the good sense to start the record over? They couldn't fire her for one bad square-dance performance, could they?

Maybe the panties were my imagination. No, a wider step confirmed their placement, still about thigh high. Trying to feel the top of the waistband through 10 inches of petticoat netting, I tugged at them casually, hoping that the host of parents in the surrounding bleachers had their eyes on somebody else.

"Give me your hand; give me your hand," Marvin ordered me. I had other things to do with my left hand. I kept groping for the elastic band with my thumb and forefinger but couldn't catch hold of anything but yards of crinoline. Without being obvious, that is. My attention was divided three ways: the feel of the slipping cloth, the feel of the audience's eyes around me, and the push and shove of my partners whispering contradictory directions, "Now left. No, here's where we swing our partners to the right."

The needle jumped to still another new cadence. One of the couples seemed to have a sense of what pattern we should be doing; so the rest of us tried to anticipate the next move and get in step.

The panties slid to my knees.

Tears welled up in my eyes. Marvin and the rest of the boys were beginning to consider this horseplay. He yanked me after him in the circle going left. "Why are you crying? It's not our fault. Vincent and Carolyn are the ones going in the wrong direction."

Couldn't he see what was happening? Then the thought occurred to me that my skirt length was midcalf; maybe the panties didn't show yet! No one was pointing. Should I pull away from the circle and try to make it offstage? But if I stopped skipping around the circle, the panties would fall even faster. If I could just keep the steps wide enough to keep the elastic pulled tight. . . .

The song seemed to go on forever.

Trying to follow Marvin's lead as the other couples decided to grab hands, face outward, and circle the center again, I failed to maintain the stretch. The pink panties fell to the floor. I broke the circle, grabbed my panties amid the giggling classmates around me, and ran off the gym floor with the laughter of the crowd burning my ears. I ran straight into the arms of my mother, standing offstage in the wings.

I cried for two days. "No one really saw what happened," she consoled me. "It's okay. They won't tease you. I promise it's going to be all right."

"But they will. They will! I can't go back."

"They won't. You'll go back, and no one will mention it. I'll see to that." She said it with such firmness that I dared believe her.

When I returned to school, I sat in isolation with my eyes glued on the front chalkboard, afraid someone might engage me in conversation. No one did. Mrs. McGowen had promised my mother to paddle anyone who brought up the subject to my face. Only Barry Day snickered when he caught my eye. And he got a paddling. I think that was Mrs. McGowen's apology to me and my mother about the scratched record.

My mother laid down the law. To this day, no one in my family has ever mentioned that incident.

Why? The late humorist Erma Bombeck used to tell her newspaper readers of similar embarrassments almost daily. I've told friends about lost loves, financial failures, and a myriad of mistakes on the job. But not about the pink panties.

Why does even thinking about this one embarrassment still bring a blush?

I don't know yet. But I do know that most people have at least one huge sore on their psyche. There's the relationship that crumbled against all they could do to hold it together. And they wouldn't dare tell another soul the cutting remark that the leaving one uttered when breaking things off.

Or there's the "performance problem"—so labeled by the boss: that nagging accusation about attitude that won't go away. Or there's the time you spent the weekend alone and did some bizarre thing because you were depressed and never thought you'd live to tell about it. Or there was the snub from a former close friend, too painful to even think about. Or there was the time someone came between you and the one you love and gloated over the situation to your face. Or there was the time you just knew you would be the award winner at a flamboyant celebration and richly recognized for some achievement—but the honor went to someone else, and you blush to think that you even entertained the idea that you might be the one to win. Worse, you told someone you expected the honor.

Or the time you arrived at a party dressed like Little Bo Peep when everybody else looked like Cleopatra. Or the time you thought your family would surprise you with some thoughtful gesture, and they didn't even notice what you'd sacrificed for them. And you were angry that you were angry. Or the time a friend told you the gossip about you "for your own good"—gossip that was both hurtful and true.

As I said, most people have that one big huge sore on their psyche. It almost goes away. For a month. For a year. For a decade. And then some little pressure or push next to the sore spot pricks the memory and the oozing pain all over again.

Time doesn't heal all wounds; it only causes some to fester.

Only Mother's words apply the protective ointment that gradually forms the scab for all time.

❧ ❧ ❧

Get your facts first, and then you can distort them
as much as you please.

—*Mark Twain*

The trouble with being a parent is that by the time
you're experienced, you're unemployed.

—*Kreolite News*

Words that Promise

ARE YOU OUT FOR GOOD, OR JUST ON FURLOUGH?

It was much too easy, not much of a challenge at all. While his friend stood watch in the doorway, Charles slipped the grading key into his notebook. Then together they sauntered back into the hallway as if deeply engaged in reflection on Friday night's football game.

Two days later, Penny Greene distributed the graded American history exams to her class. She called her students to attention. They sat sullen, but with eyes turned toward the front.

"We . . . as a group . . . didn't do too well on this test." She pursed her lips. "I'm disappointed. The class average was seventy-five." She paused again, as if she wanted that news to sink in.

Charles caught the eye of his friend and tried to suppress a grin.

Ms. Greene continued, "However, we had two very good grades—both ninety-eights. Charles and Johnny."

Their classmates looked at them with contempt.

"Would you two boys please stand up."

It wasn't a question. Charles and Johnny stood.

"Boys, your grades, in light of the class average, seem a little surprising. Can you explain them?"

Neither answered. Charles surprised himself by his delayed response. After all, he'd been voted "Class Wit." And after his name had been placed into nomination, all other nominations ceased. Anyway, who did she think she was? After all, a 98 wasn't unusual for him. If something drastic didn't happen, he'd end the year as valedictorian. Actually, her insinuation angered him.

All eyes in the class were frozen on them. Ms. Greene repeated her question, then asked, "Did you two cheat on this test?"

Neither boy spoke.

"Johnny, I want an answer. Did you cheat on this test?"

He stammered a moment and then said, "I ain't sayin'. I ain't sayin' if I did or if I didn't."

Ms. Green cut her eyes toward Charles. "Did you cheat?"

Charles looked at his feet a moment and then looked up with a very sober face. "Yes, ma'am. I did and I'm very sorry. I apologize."

Ms. Greene looked shocked. Well, that was understandable, he thought. He had created so much grief for her, along with every other teacher he'd ever had, that his words might have been perceived as insincere. He certainly didn't want that, so he decided to repeat them—in his most sincere voice.

"Yes, ma'am. I'm *really sorry* I did that," he paused a little longer for effect, "because I could've made 98 on that test— without cheating *or* studying."

The whole class burst out laughing.

But as he and Johnny took their seats, he felt a twinge of guilt for having outdone Ms. Greene once again. Well, okay, he argued with himself, she was a decent person, but she just had no sense of humor. She should know better than to tangle with him and Johnny. The other school officials had learned their lesson long ago.

A few months later, he decided that this little skirmish shouldn't keep him from asking her to sign his yearbook. So he handed it to her and stood there sheepishly while she wrote. Later that day, he flipped it open to read these words: "Charles, you're a very smart student. You're a leader, and you have great potential. I'm expecting the best from you. Just always remember this: To know God's will is the greatest knowledge; to do it, life's greatest achievement."

He closed the yearbook. Sounded like a teacher. She went to church, he knew that. But she shouldn't ever expect him to be there. He'd never darkened a church door in Vivian, Louisiana, and he didn't intend to start now. "The greatest knowledge?" He was smart; his grades proved it. What did God have to do with "achievement"?

It wasn't until Charles's conversion at the age of twenty-six that he understood the truth of those words. The intervening years had been more of the same attitude that he'd exhibited that day in Ms. Greene's classroom. He'd thumbed his nose at God as well as Ms. Greene, sure that he could make it on his own wit and wisdom.

On a visit back to Vivian for his tenth high school reunion, he discovered that most of his former classmates remembered his cocky demeanor. One of them stuck out his hand and greeted Charles with this comment: "Are you out for good, or just on furlough?"

Charles Thornton is now the minister of evangelism at First Baptist Church, Euless, Texas, one of the largest Protestant churches in the nation. He travels extensively to speak around the country and has his own syndicated radio broadcast called "New Life for You."

Ms. Penny Greene recently had occasion to drive to Vivian, Louisiana, to hear Charles preach in his hometown—the first and only time he has ever attended worship services there. With the same confidence, minus the cockiness, he had the opportunity to agree with her: "To know God's will is the greatest knowledge; to do it, life's greatest achievement."

✤ ✤ ✤

A gentle answer turns away wrath, but a harsh word stirs up anger.

—*Proverbs 15:1*

Pray also for me, that whenever I open my mouth, words may be given me so that I will fearlessly make known the mystery of the gospel.

—*Ephesians 6:19*

Words that Delay

I'VE BEEN MEANING TO DO THAT

*B*eautiful and vivacious, Alexia rose from the sofa and introduced herself to me as I joined her and her husband in the lobby of a grand hotel in San Francisco. "Would you like some pink lemonade?" she asked as she gestured toward a table near the concierge's desk. "I wouldn't offer to get it for you if you were a man," she laughed easily, "but for you, I'll do the honors."

I thanked her and she disappeared, leaving me to get better acquainted with her husband, Garrett, a senior consultant with one of the major accounting firms in the country. He was the epitome of the straight-laced, distinguished financier—just enough gray at the temples to be wise and just enough twinkle in the eye to be trustworthy. Garrett and I chatted a minute, mostly about the new love of his life, until she rejoined us. His wife was a thirty-something psychologist in Boston with a large corporate clientele. She had accompanied him on this trip to meet with CEOs about mergers, acquisitions, and roll-ups within the industry.

Before I consider doing business with someone, I like to get to know him or her personally, so I asked Garrett, "Tell me, do you two get to travel together all the time?"

"Often," he said, reaching over to pat Alexia's knee. "Mostly during the week, however, because many of her corporate clients do their counseling sessions by telephone."

"Oh, really. That's interesting."

"Yeah, so we get to travel a lot during the week. Plus I do some preaching on the side."

"That's a great combination. Where?"

"No particular place. I just do fill-ins here and there. Several things in South America."

"Alexia, do you get to go with him to South America when he preaches?"

"Sometimes," she said. "Actually, I've kind of gotten away from all that spiritual emphasis. I went to church, that sort of thing, when I was a child. But ever since Garrett and I married a couple of years ago, I've been meaning to get back to all that."

To Garrett, I said, "My faith's a very important part of my life. I'm really glad to know that about you."

The conversation drifted to something else before we parted half an hour later to attend the opening gala of the three-day meeting.

Later that evening, I watched them together as they mixed and mingled at the party. Introducing her to his business associates with pride, he obviously adored her. She wore a sequined black gown that drew attention as she glided from one group to the next. She laughed easily and seemed to find no difficulty in holding her own in each conversation. As she recounted story after story of their travels together, she grew more and more animated. The thought occurred to me that she had superior sales skills to Garrett's. In my brief half-hour assessment,

I'd confirmed for myself that she was indeed a bright and gracious woman. I hoped that she'd soon have time to "get back to all that" where the spiritual was concerned.

From time to time during the next three months, I saw them together at major industry meetings. And on more than one occasion, when someone asked Garrett about his preaching activities, she had no comment of her own to add. Instead, she stood quietly until he finished his tale and then moved on to the latest escapade or corporate project in her own life.

About a year after our initial meeting, Garrett stopped by our trade show booth alone and spoke to my husband.

Vernon shook his hand and said, "Well, I haven't seen you in a while."

"You're right," he said, "I've missed a few events during the past six months. I just returned from a preaching tour in Brazil."

"Great. How did it go? How have you been?"

"Not good," he said. The twinkle was gone from his eyes. Instead, they filled with tears. He turned his face away to regain his composure. Then he turned back to Vernon, "Alexia died three weeks ago. Breast cancer."

When my husband later told me of their conversation, my first thought was of Alexia's comment: "I've been meaning to get back to all that." I pray that she did.

☙ ☙ ☙

"Ask and it will be given to you; seek and you will find; knock and the door will be opened to you."
—*Matthew 7:7*

Words that Prove

A LONG, LONG WALK

The medical missionary in Kenya glanced up to see a bedraggled woman knocking at his lab door. It was after hours, and he had turned off the outdoor lights to discourage the people from interrupting him. When there was so much need, what difference could a few more hours of waiting make to those who spent most of their life waiting for someone to come to their aid?

He berated himself for the callous thought, then corrected himself. No, it was just that he had their long-term welfare in mind. The hours he stole for himself in the early evening were for continuing his research. Maybe it was wishful thinking, but he believed he was on the right track with a mysterious African disease for which there was no cure at present.

The woman kept knocking. The doctor put down his test tube, took off his lab jacket, and shuffled to the door. He flipped the switch and flooded the front yard with light. He opened the door to the African woman.

"May I help you?"

"I brought you a gift," was all she said. She held out a basketful of herbs.

"What are these?"

"I heard you speak when you were in our village last week. You said you needed more herbs for your research." The doctor searched his mind for the location and the comment. The woman had called the roots by a different name, the common term, but the doctor immediately recognized them as the rare herbs he'd referred to in his talk the previous week.

"I found them," the woman repeated. "This is the one you wanted?"

Astonished, the doctor grabbed the basket from her. "Yes! Yes! Thank you. Thank you. Yes, I needed more. But . . ." he looked down at the woman's dusty, torn sandals. Her forehead and arms glistened with sweat in the light. "But how did you get *here?*"

"I walked."

"But your village is more than thirty miles away!"

"Yes." The woman smiled. "That's part of the gift."

∞ ∞ ∞

"And I will do whatever you ask in my name, so that the Son may bring glory to the Father."

—*John 14:13*

Words that Cheer

WHO WANTS TO BE *NORMAL?*

*A*s a performer in her local community theater, Lilly Walters is passionate about her voice. So when her throat became very sore during a particularly grueling show run, she became terrified that she had done damage to her vocal cords. As lead in the opera, she was determined to get her throat problem corrected immediately.

When her family doctor kept her waiting for her appointment for more than an hour, she left in a huff, went back to her office, grabbed a phone book, and called a nearby throat specialist. She made a second appointment.

The nurse asked her to take a seat and wait. Again. Lilly was rarely sick, and here she was just before the big opera, off work and waiting. Disgruntled, she harrumphed and shuffled when the nurse finally escorted her back into the examination room and closed the door.

After a moment, the nurse stepped back into the room and said, "May I ask you something personal?"

Lilly looked up. "Yes, of course." The question was rather

odd. What other kinds of questions did they ask you in a doctor's office but "personal" ones?

"I noticed your hand," the nurse said hesitantly.

Lilly was a little taken aback. Not that she minded being asked about her hand, but simply by the fact that someone had noticed it at all. She had lost half of her hand in a forklift accident at the age of eleven. But she'd so often heard the comment, "Gee, your hand—I never noticed that before," from friends that she sometimes forgot she had only a thumb and a stub on her left hand. From the first day she'd tried out for a comedy at the local community theater, she was routinely cast in almost every production. The partially missing hand had not been an issue.

"What I need to know," the nurse continued, "is how it has affected your life."

Never in all the years since the accident had anyone asked her such a question. Yes, others had asked whether it bothered her, but never had she heard such a sweeping question as this.

After an awkward pause, the nurse continued, "I just had a baby, and her hand is like yours. I . . . well . . . I need to know how it has affected your life."

"How has it affected my life?" Lilly turned the question over in her mind. She wanted to think of just the right words. The pain was raw on the nurse's face.

Finally, Lilly said, "It has affected my life—but not in a bad way. I do many things that people with two normal hands find difficult. I type about seventy-five words a minute. I play guitar. I have ridden and shown horses for years. I even have a horsemaster degree. I'm involved in musical theater, and I am a professional speaker. I'm constantly in front of a crowd. I do television shows four or five times a year."

The nurse's eyes widened as if to take in what she was hearing.

Lilly continued, "I think it was never 'difficult' because of the love and encouragement of my family. They always talked about all the great notoriety I would get because I would learn how to do things with one hand that most people had trouble doing with two. We were all very excited about that. That was the main focus—not the handicap.

"Your daughter does not have a problem. She is normal. You are the one who will teach her to think of herself as anything else. She will come to know she is 'different,' but you will teach her that 'different' is wonderful. Normal means you are average. What's fun about that?"

The nurse stood silently for a while, examining Lilly's face as if to siphon the truth from the words she had heard. Then she said simply, "Thank you," and walked out of the room.

Shortly, the doctor came in to look at Lilly's throat. "I'm going to need to anesthetize your throat to put a probe down it so I can examine you."

Not my throat, you don't, she thought. I'm singing in an opera tomorrow night. She thanked him just the same and left his office without the examination.

The next day her throat was fine.

☙ ☙ ☙

We are all pencils in the hands of God.
                                                —*Mother Theresa*

An anxious heart weighs a man down, but a kind word cheers him up.
                                                —*Proverbs 12:25*

A large part of this story was written by Lilly Walters.

Words that Praise

PICKING EGGS

When my granddaddy was sixty, he stopped his pickup truck on the highway to wait for an approaching car before making a left-hand turn onto the gravel road that led to his farm. An eighteen-wheeler hit him from behind. The impact of the collision sent him through the front window onto the pavement.

For months he lay in the hospital, in critical condition with multiple internal injuries. Each day my grandmother drove to sit at his side from early morning until late night. Then one morning, she didn't show up at the hospital. Worried, the nurses called her daughters, who'd also been almost daily visitors, to inquire about Mrs. Schronk.

My aunt drove out to the farmhouse about noon and found my grandmother unconscious on the bathroom floor. She was diagnosed with cancer of the colon. Shortly thereafter, her doctors discovered that the cancer had spread to her brain.

When I visited her a week before she fell into a coma from which she never recovered, I persuaded the nurses to let me take my four-month-old son, her second great grandchild, with me. I held him up near the bed so she could see him. She tried to chuck his chin, but her formerly sturdy arms were too weak to reach him. Instead, she smiled broadly and tried to gurgle back at him.

The sight of them together carried me back to my own childhood when I'd spent many two- and three-day "vacations" on her farm. When my mother drove me there, I could hardly wait until the car came to a complete stop before I'd jump out and run inside. "When can we go pick eggs?" I'd ask.

"Later. Later," she always promised with a wink. "Just as soon as we can get your mother out the door and on her way. You'd better go tell her to hurry—that us girls have a lot to talk about."

Then I'd impatiently wait for Mother to leave so I could be the center of my grandmother's attention. Never mind the baked bread and canned pears. Despite her rotund figure, she sat on the floor to play marbles with me. And when she got tickled at some antic of mine, her whole body shook. Sometimes she laughed so long and hard that she had to sit down to keep from falling down. She offered her coal-black hair in my rocking chair "beauty parlor." When we played doctor, she gladly offered her arms for shots and slings and surgery.

We never made the early-morning or late-afternoon route through the hen house to "pick eggs" that she didn't pronounce, "Well, I'll declare—look at those eggs. Those chickens never lay that many eggs until you come for a visit." And when she tucked us into the center of the big feather bed at night, I dozed off to sleep with the lingering smell of her dusty rose talc powder.

I still stood watching her enjoy the baby's cooing on the side of her hospital bed that day. It seemed like only months rather than years since the day of her older brother's funeral. She'd had her routine winter bout of bronchitis, and her doctor wouldn't let her go out in the cold air to travel to the funeral. She baby-sat us kids while the rest of the family attended the funeral. Too young to understand her sorrow, we whooped and hollered at her feet.

But I did overhear her take a phone call late that day. The friend must have been offering her condolences because I remember being alarmed at seeing Grandmother cry for the first time. "The Good Lord said He wouldn't put on us more than we could bear."

As my tiny son continued to coo beside her hospital bed, a friend stopped by for a brief moment. When her friend commented on her unfortunate circumstances—her lying sick in one hospital and my grandfather lying injured in another hospital across town—my grandmother's comment was simply, "The Good Lord told us He'd never put on us more than we can bear."

That was the last time my grandmother saw her great grandbaby and the last time I saw her conscious. As she slipped into a coma and died, my grandfather's body healed.

His mind did not.

Grandmother never lived to learn that Granddad had to be placed in a mental asylum for the last two years of his life. And he, likewise, never understood that she had become ill and died.

At her graveside, her brother-in-law stopped by to comfort my mother and aunts. He leaned down and rested his elbow on the window of our funeral car, took a long draw on his cigar, and then made only one comment: "I've been in the family for a long, long time. . . . And I've known Anna for many, many years. As far as I can remember, I've never heard her say one negative thing about nobody . . ."

He took another puff on his cigar. "You can't say that about many people these days."

He turned and sauntered toward her grave to pay his last respects.

☙ ☙ ☙

"But I tell you that men will have to give account on the day of judgment for every careless word they have spoken."

—*Matthew 12:36*

Praise the name of the Lord your God, who has worked wonders for you.

—*Joel 2:26*

Give thanks in all circumstances, for this is God's will for you in Christ Jesus.

—*1 Thessalonians 5:18*

Words that Determine

During an autographing session in Houston recently, I met a woman by the name of Diana Ramsey. She was a delightful woman, with an infectious smile and wonderful sense of humor. I had heard her chatting with a couple of sales associates on the floor and had gathered that she must be a regular in their department store.

Then she sauntered over to my book table. First she purchased a copy of *Ten Smart Moves for Women* for me to autograph. Then she said, "Might as well get another copy of that for my daughter. She's just finishing her Ph.D. in education."

"Oh, congratulations. I'll just make this a congratulatory note to her inside the cover. That okay?"

"That'll be good," she nodded. I began to autograph the second copy to her daughter.

She paused while I wrote, took the book from me, and started to move on. Then suddenly she turned back to me. "Oh . . . you might as well just give me a copy of that one too." She pointed to a third book.

"Sure thing." I picked up a copy from the next pile, opened it, and paused for her next direction.

"Make that to my other daughter. She's an attorney, and I'm sure she'd be interested in anything on oral presentation skills." She gave me the name of her second daughter, and I began to autograph the third book.

She picked up the next book off the display and handed it to me. "This *Communicate with Confidence*—make it to my son. He's a medical doctor. I know more than a few doctors who could use better communication skills."

I agreed and autographed the fourth book.

She picked up a fifth title, "Autograph this one to my son, the architect." She gave me his name while I scribbled inside the book cover.

"That's quite an accomplishment," I said to her, after signing the last book and handing it back to her. "Four children grown and so well-educated."

She smiled modestly.

"I'm serious. In this day and age, just to have them all speaking to you at the same time can be a real feat. You and your husband must have really placed a lot of emphasis on the value of education. Tell me, how did you do it?"

She laughed. "Well, here's what I always told them. I said to them, 'You like this lifestyle that we live? Well, it costs money. You can either earn it or steal it. And I suggest that you earn it— you get to keep it that way.'" She let go another chuckle.

The line obviously worked.

∾ ∾ ∾

The thought manifests as the word. The word manifests
as the deed. Deeds form into habits. And habits harden
into character. So watch your thoughts with care.
　　　　　　　　　　　　　　　　—*Thomas Merton*

Words that Model

PLAYING PING-PONG SOBER

Kerry leaned over the Ping-Pong table and slammed the ball into the opposite corner. His dad missed the return by a full foot. But even when his dad was drunk, Kerry had to concede, he was a good player.

"New game," his dad said, retrieving the ball from beneath the power saw in the corner of their garage.

"Are you sure, Dad?"

"Yeah, I'm sure. New game," he demanded.

Kerry had him down four games for the afternoon. On a one-case day, his dad could still hold his own in their tournaments; on a one-and-a-half case day, Kerry definitely had the upper hand.

The thing was, Kerry loved his dad. Despite the arguing, despite his dad's temper, despite the man's rudeness and burly attitude, despite his embarrassment when one of his friends dropped by, Kerry still loved him.

His mother set the tone for their relationship. At eighteen, Kerry battled the urge to show his dad the door. After all, by

most people's standards, Kerry was also a man. With graduation only a few months away, he had a job lined up. In fact,
he planned to go into business for himself. Doing just what,
he hadn't quite decided, but he felt capable of taking care of
his own future. His dad, sober or drunk, could no longer
wreck his future.

His mother shouted through the back door over their ruckus
in the garage. "Dinner's about ready. You've got ten minutes."

His daddy cursed at the ball as he swung again and
missed. "Ten to seven," Kerry called the score and continued
his serve. Many nights he'd seen his dad come into the house
in a drunken stupor and curse his mother over some little
wrong, either real or imagined. She would shake her head, put
her hands on her hips, and raise her voice at him, "Herman,
I'm about to lose my patience with you."

Kerry cracked a smile just thinking about her "strong"
stance. When his dad had done something particularly obnox-
ious, his mother would say more loudly, "Herman, I'm really
about to lose my patience with you."

But she never did.

That was the thing.

That was the thing that Kerry saw day after day after day.
She stayed. She prayed. She pouted. She doubted. She hoped.
She watched. But she always stayed.

"Eighteen to twelve," Kerry called the score.

His dad slurred, "Are you sure? That was off the table,
kiddo."

"Nope, it hit the corner."

His dad slapped his paddle on his thigh, threw back his
head, and laughed.

Kerry served again. He remembered the one and only time
he'd seen his mother angry enough to have the luggage open
on the bed. But when he'd walked into the room and asked

her where she was going, she'd simply said, "Nowhere, I guess. But I'm about to lose my patience with your dad." She had put the bags away.

And she never let him show disrespect to his father. That was the strongest lesson. "Your dad's going to stop his drinking one day, and you two need to have a good relationship. He's still your dad."

"Even if you're about to lose your patience?" Kerry had mimicked her during one of their heated discussions over his behavior.

She'd responded, "I haven't lost it yet. He's your father; don't forget that."

"Game." Kerry said matter-of-factly and put down the paddle. He tried to sift the frustration from his voice; in his mother's words, he was about to lose his patience.

"Come on," his dad said, "let's go another one."

"Look, I already beat you six games today."

"Only reason you're whipping me is 'cause I'm drunk. You play me someday when I'm not drunk."

"Dad, . . . when would that be? You're drunk every day."

His dad dropped the paddle back on the table and stared at him for a long moment.

"I guess you're right," he said as he swaggered over to sit on the steps.

Kerry disappeared into the house for dinner. It was the closest he'd come in a long time to confronting his dad. Respectful? Would his mother have called that respectful? He thought it over as he washed his hands and combed his hair for dinner. He looked himself squarely in the mirror. He'd said nothing but the truth—the angry, hard truth. But then, he was about to lose his patience.

His dad didn't come into the house for dinner that night. But he never touched another bottle of beer.

✍ ✍ ✍

Remember that quiet patience can and does master
and outlive all boisterous, stormy human discords.
—*Lowell Filmore*

An honest answer is like a kiss on the lips.
—*Proverbs 24:26*

Words that Love

WHO SAID I DIDN'T NOTICE?

This letter poem was written by seventeen year-old Jenivie Isgitt to her mother, Karen Rinehart, on Mother's Day.

THANKS FOR EVERYTHING, MOM

Thank you for always giving me a second chance.
Thank you for telling me to read the fine print before I sign
  anything.
Thank you for not taking off the training wheels until I asked.
Thank you for smearing sunblock all over my face.
Thank you for being just as surprised as I was at six A.M. on
  Christmas.
Thank you for always including me in the conversation at the
  dinner table.
Thank you for not buying me everything I asked for.
Thank you for making me wear my seat belt.
Thank you for accepting my collect calls.
Thank you for letting me stay up late to watch the end of a
  movie.

Thank you for not finding me within the first few seconds when we played a game of hide-and-seek.

Thank you for riding with me when I got my driver's permit.

Thank you for reading my favorite book over and over.

Thank you for letting me stay home from school even when I was only a little bit sick.

Thank you for ordering my school pictures.

Thank you for driving me to the movies and then picking me up again.

Thank you for buying Valentine's Day cards for everyone in my class.

Thank you for not letting "everyone's doing it" be a good enough reason.

Thank you for not saying, "You ask too many questions!"

Thank you for warm clothes right out of the dryer.

Thank you for thinking the weeds I picked for you were beautiful.

Thank you for always displaying the cards I made you.

Thank you for always inviting my friends to stay for dinner.

Thank you for showing me I was wrong when I insisted there was nothing to do on a rainy day.

Thank you for being there whenever I needed you the most.

❧ ❧ ❧

I like not only to be loved, but to be told that I am loved; the realm of silence is large enough beyond the grave.

—*George Eliot (pseudonym for Mary Ann Evans)*

Words that Challenge

DON'T BE WHAT I WANT YOU TO BE

The couple sat stiffly on the sofa in their marriage counselor's office once again. For six long months, they'd been coming to this woman for help in spicing up or pouring out this pot of boiling stew they both felt they were swimming in.

On this particular day, the counselor decided to start with a summary of the ingredients that both had shared that made the marriage so miserable.

"Tina, you've told me that you feel ignored. That you feel Jim doesn't listen to you, doesn't care about you or your son. That he tries to distance himself from you, doesn't tell you what he's thinking, doesn't discuss decisions with you, doesn't ever appreciate what you do around the house, doesn't compliment you. . . . You resent his interest in pornography. . . . You're disappointed and frustrated that both of you overspend and then argue too much about money. You think he—"

"Wait a minute, she—" Jim started in.

"Please let me finish. I'm just summing up as a place to start today."

He snorted and slouched back on the sofa.

The counselor continued, "You feel there's no closeness in your relationship—that you're living your life in the same house but that's about all. Does that about sum up what you've told me these past months?"

Tina nodded and her eyes filled with tears again. "It's not *all* true anymore—not the part about living in the same house. I moved out this week. I took Kyle, and we got our own apartment."

"I see," said the counselor. "And was there anything particular that pushed you to that decision?"

Jim leaned forward again, "Yeah. She started in with all the accusations again, and I told her to shut up, that I was tired of listening to her whine and complain. She's on my back constantly about something."

"So let me finish my summary then, Jim."

He shrugged in her direction.

"You, Jim, told me that you agree that both of you overspend for things you don't need. You say the pornographic magazines and movies don't have anything to do with the problems in the marriage—that you can take them or leave them. You feel that Tina demands too much from you and tries to monopolize your time, that she won't let you have your own life and make your own decisions. Do I hear you right—is that what you've told me about how you feel?"

"Look," Jim said, "I'm not arguing that I need to do some changing."

Tina stuffed her Kleenex in her pocket and looked his way.

His voice softened as he went on, "I want to be what she wants me to be. I want to be there for her. I want to be more sensitive to her and Kyle. I want to listen to her and make her happy. I want to be the committed husband she expects me to be. I want to be what she thinks—"

"Stop, stop right there," the marriage counselor interrupted. "You'll never make any change as long as it's for *her*. You'll never make those changes permanently unless you make them for *you*. You'll have to take ownership. *You* personally have to want to be those things—because that's the kind of person *you yourself* want to be."

He looked at her as if addled by a two-by-four between the eyes.

They continued the session, but Jim heard nothing more that day.

Two months later, Jim and Tina moved back in together. According to Jim, those words from the counselor served as the turning point in their marriage.

✐   ✐   ✐

Motivation is the art of getting people to do what you want them to do because they want to do it.
　　　　　　　　　　　　—*Dwight Eisenhower*

Words that Gossip

IT'S TRUE—JUST GO ASK YOUR MOTHER

Almost twenty years ago, I noticed a red circle about two inches in diameter on my breast. When it didn't go away, I made an appointment with my gynecologist.

"Frankly, I don't know what it is. There's a very rare form of cancer that makes a red mark like that. But I usually see that on a diabetic, and the spot usually appears somewhere on the leg. At your age, breast cancer is so rare. I'm going to hope it's an infection of some kind and put you on antibiotics for a month to see if it goes away."

So I left his office with a month to twiddle my thumbs. To keep my mind occupied, I focused on grad school two days a week and finishing the book I had under contract. In my spare time, I tried to keep the house clean, meals cooked, and get my six-year-old and eight-year-old to school, piano lessons, and soccer practice.

Outside of telling my church friends so they could pray, I had little time for visiting. But I noticed occasionally that two of my neighbors gathered at their mailboxes each day about the same time.

The weeks dragged by. I tried to stay busy and confident.

I reported to the doctor again for another examination. He remained undecided about whether a biopsy was in order. He wanted to try another medication first and asked me to return for another examination four weeks later.

I waited. I studied. I wrote. I washed. I watched ball games.

Then one afternoon as I was in the middle of making dinner, I heard both kids come running into the house from the backyard. I kept at my task at the kitchen counter without turning around to interrupt their play. Thinking they had whizzed on past me down the hall to their bedrooms, I turned around suddenly to get something from the refrigerator and nearly fell over them.

Both were standing there, staring at me. Tears streamed down their faces.

"What's the matter?" I asked. "What happened?"

Neither answered me. They just stared and let the tears roll.

"Jeff, Lisa, answer me. Are you hurt? What's the matter?"

"Tina's mother said you have cancer. She said you're going to die."

"No, no, no." I swept them into my arms and held them tightly.

"Why would she say that to you?" It wasn't a question I intended for them, but for her.

Lisa wiped at her wet cheeks. "Tina said she heard her mother telling her friends on the telephone. She said you were going to die—soon. She said it was true—to go ask my mother."

"No, honey. She's mistaken. She doesn't know anything about it. I don't know why she would say something like that. But it's not true."

It was all I could do to keep from running out of the house, stalking next door, and shaking my neighbor by the shoulders. I recalled other tidbits of newsy information she and her friends had passed on in my presence: Whose kids in the neighborhood were failing at school. Whose husband had run away with his secretary. Whose kids were "probably" dealing drugs. Which teachers were "incompetent." Which women didn't know "diddly-squat" about running the home-owners' association. Which builders were going bankrupt. Which wife was sleeping around and how little her "stupid" husband knew.

But this. Certainly, she could have been more careful with this "news."

It took me half an hour to explain the situation to the children—a chore I had hoped not to have to do until I knew we were taking some sort of decisive action. I had never intended the kids to endure the long wait with their father and me.

Subsequently, I did get a second opinion, had to have a biopsy, and then discovered that the mass in my breast was benign. But every week for the next four years that we lived in that neighborhood, I watched the pair of women gather on my neighbor's front lawn and "visit."

It occurred to me more than once that other subjects of their gossip had not fared so well.

❧ ❧ ❧

A dog is smarter than some people. It wags its tail and not its tongue.

—*Unknown*

Gossip has never been put in the same bag as mur-

der and assassination, but it is in the same family.
Gossip assassinates a person's character.

—*C. Neil Strait*

It seems a misnomer to call it idle gossip when it's
always doing a job on somebody.

—*Unknown*

Gossip is always a personal confession of either
malice or imbecility—shun it.

—*J. G. Holland*

A gossip separates close friends.

—*Proverbs 16:28*

Words *that* Motivate

FIRST THING MONDAY MORNING

*N*ever buy a car built on Mondays or Fridays. You've probably heard that sentiment from those aware of the fact that employees seldom do their best work on those days.

But the problem is not always the day of the week; it's often the person we greet.

"I was squeaking by with a C in algebra and feeling very lost," says Polly Fuhrman of her ninth-grade year, her first in a public school after having attended a Catholic school for the previous years. She was tossed into the whole new experience of changing classrooms and teachers on the hour and mingling with a very diverse student body.

"I'm afraid I didn't like Ms. Haung, my algebra teacher, because she was strict. Also she had a quirky sense of humor and would say things like, 'Have a happy, mathy, weekend' and such. Looking back now, I'm sure it was that I was in that early teenage, cynical, all-adults-are-out-of-touch phase. But I didn't like her. Then one day she pulled me aside after class and said, 'Polly, I've seen your standardized test scores and they show a high math aptitude. For some reason, you're not working up to your potential. How much time are you spending on algebra?'

"I don't know how I answered her that day, but the truth was 'none.' Up until that point, my schoolwork had come with little effort. But her comment and question to me told me that my secret was out of the bag—I knew that she knew I was smart enough to do the work. I went from a C that first marking period to A's for the rest of the year in both algebra and biology."

Such has been the influence of motivational teachers.

There are the Mrs. McCulloughs of the world: "Diagramming sentences is fun. We're going to make a game of it. Okay, everybody, go to the board, and then we'll divide into teams and appoint a scorekeeper." That was her way of ratcheting up the energy after lunch in our class of seventh graders who never thought they'd have to understand sentence structure to write an engineering report.

There are the Mrs. Jennings of the world: "Lisa has been giving me a bit of trouble in class. I'm calling to solicit your and her father's help to change that behavior. I've got a group of girls who're creating a disturbance by giggling and doing everything in class but their work. Lisa's a real leader. She's popular, and she can have a big influence on her classmates. That's why I called you first. I'd like to see if you have any ideas that would help me motivate her in this class."

A real leader? What a tactful way to phrase the problem to a parent. Sure, we can turn that little problem around. And we did.

Finally, there are the Miss Amoses of the world. They stand in a class all their own.

The first day I walked into her American literature class,

I was scared. Not because of the subject or the fact that this was my first day in a new school in a new class of 465 students in a new city.

I was frightened by her face. Her nose was, well, huge and curved sharply toward the left cheekbone. Big black bags hung under piercing dark eyes. Her silver hair gave the strongest evidence that she had paid some serious attention to her appearance. It was parted perfectly straight and combed flat down to her ears, then held in place by a tight roll of pin curls around the edges. Below her neck, everything else seemed normal, wrapped in a smartly tailored dress. But her face—I couldn't take my eyes off her face.

I took my seat and slid around to look at her squarely. She silently wrote on the chalkboard behind her in big bold print: "MISS AMOS." Then turning back to face us, she said, "You'll notice there's no period after the 'Miss'—that makes it all too final. I'm still hoping."

The class laughed uneasily, and that began my year with Miss Amos.

By the third week in September, her bulletin board was completely lined with white mums and green ribbons, each sprouting a glittering number in the center. Two days before the homecoming game, the bulletin board had mums three rows deep inside the flowered frame. Her explanation? Former students sent them "just because."

In October a burly football player sauntered into class late, mumbling apologies about oversleeping. She cleared her throat and harrumphed, "Chris, if you're sleeping more than three hours a night, you're sleeping your life away."

He slid into his seat sheepishly. But as she surveyed the room with her piercing stare, the comment was not lost on the rest of us.

It was obviously a principle she lived by. No matter what the length of the essays we handed in, she returned them the next day—graded. "It's important that you get immediate feedback. I want you to see your errors immediately so you can correct them before the next paper. Errors have ways of becoming habits."

In November, we read Edgar Allan Poe. Dated? Of course not. Our assignment was to read two current mysteries or spy thrillers and compare each author's techniques to the spine-tingling techniques Poe had pioneered.

"When I was reading this morning . . . at 2:00 A.M.," she said, pausing for effect, "I decided that those of you who like horror movies would probably want to read this novel before the movie comes out. Yes, it will definitely become a movie—and don't forget that I was the first to let you know."

So that was obviously the cause of the permanent black circles on her face—reading and grading papers at all hours of the night. I made another mental note—she obviously stayed up to date. Unlike other English teachers I'd known, maybe she did actually read books written after World War II.

Maybe she did, after all, understand teenage love. I'd noticed her watching me through her doorway several mornings as I walked the halls with my "friend" Mike.

"So you and Mike are steady now?" she asked me one day when I walked into her classroom early.

"We're friends. That's all." I blushed. Teachers didn't understand the rules about boyfriends and just friends.

She gave me her impish grin. "You could do worse than Mike. He's in my sixth period. You two make a nice couple." And her attention was back to her papers.

I made another mental note. She obviously understood

that kids had things in their lives more important than Emerson, Thoreau, and dangling participles.

In December she attended all our school programs: the choir concert on the city square, the band benefit for new uniforms, and the various toy drives sponsored by the school clubs.

In January I quietly slipped up to her desk before the bell rang to ask if she'd review my outline for the research paper that was to be a huge chunk of our semester grade. I hated to interrupt her concentration, but I needed an answer before the weekend.

"Would you please take a minute to approve my outline now? I'm sorry; I know you told us you'd do that in class next Tuesday. But I sort of have this scheduling problem."

She peered at me over her glasses, waiting for me to spit it out—why I wasn't sticking by the project plan and due dates she'd outlined to lead us through this first harrowing research experience.

I explained to her pencil-arched gray eyebrows. "I've got a part-time job at Sears, and I never know what hours I'm going to have to work from week to week. But I wanted to start on my paper this weekend while I have a little time."

She pulled my outline to her, gave it a quick review, wrote "approved" at the top, and initialed it. I breathed a sigh of relief.

As the bell rang and I was returning to my seat, she said to the class, "Dianna just brought her outline in for me to approve it—early." She paused, waiting for the class's attention. "She didn't want to wait until the last minute." Again, she let her lighthearted, sardonic comment hang in the air before continuing.

"A few students . . . do . . . tend . . . to procrastinate," she paused again for effect. Then she deadpanned, "Of course, I realize that she probably has a lot more time on her hands than most of you—since she's only working twenty hours a week at a part-time job. Nevertheless, just a word to the wise—I'll be glad to okay your outline at any point you see fit to hand it to me."

Then she opened her literature book and took her place at the lectern in front of us.

I slid down into my seat, mortified. Everyone in the class would hate me. Why had she done that? Didn't she know better than to tell the others I was early?

But later, I reflected on her praise. So she had noticed and appreciated my time-management skills? Her approbation sank deeper. So somebody besides my parents thought time management important?

I hardly noticed her nose anymore.

In March she announced career day in her class. Each of us had to prepare a talk on three occupations that we might want to pursue. Carol, a classmate, had selected "flight attendant" as one of her careers. After she finished her overview of opportunities in flying, Miss Amos posed this question to her: "So tell me, what would you do if I as a passenger got drunk on one of your flights?"

Carol shrugged. "Drunk? I don't know. I don't know what the rules are about that," she stammered.

"So how do you feel about serving liquor? Haven't I heard you say you and your parents don't approve of drinking?"

"Yes, ma'am. That's right."

"If that's part of your basic value system, how could you in good conscience serve me liquor until I got drunk?"

"Well, I guess then maybe I wouldn't," Carol again attempted an answer.

"Are you saying you'd *not* fulfill the job responsibilities your employer asked you to do?"

"Well, I guess then I'd . . . well, I guess I'd have to ask my supervisor."

"So what would you do if that supervisor asked you to put your customer on an unsafe plane?" and with that question, Miss Amos proceeded to turn the discussion into an ethics issue about personal responsibility.

She did that often. Whether all 132 of her students agreed or not, there was no doubt they knew where she stood on issues. Her basic conclusion: Morality wasn't relative to the situation and the people involved. Life was composed of right and wrong choices.

By May, Miss Amos had taught us to plan, to research, to speak, to write, and to think. I'm still drawing from the well she dug in my life. My only regret—she died before I told her.

❧ ❧ ❧

The mediocre teacher tells. The good teacher explains. The superior teacher demonstrates. The great teacher inspires.

—*William A. Ward*

Words that Judge

CAN YOU IMAGINE THAT?

On day five of my grandson's life, he had to be hospitalized for vomiting and severe diarrhea. Doctors started testing for the biggies: *E. coli* and spinal meningitis. Both my daughter and son-in-law stayed with him for two straight days and nights in the hospital.

To complicate the situation, my son-in-law had just started a new job as youth minister for a local church. When he called in to the church secretary to get his messages and speak to the pastor, he asked whether he should leave the hospital and come in to work. The pastor assured him that he should stay with his wife and baby during this critical period, mentioning that he'd had only one call from a church member about his absence.

The woman had phoned the pastor earlier that morning demanding: "Where's Kevin?" Before the pastor could respond, she continued, "I just phoned his office and learned he's not in. And he wasn't in yesterday either. Twelve days on the job and he's taking a vacation—already? I wish I had that kind of job."

"I understand," the pastor responded. "Actually, he's at the hospital today. His newborn was readmitted. They're testing for spinal meningitis."

"Oh."

When I heard the story, my first thought was that the caller probably wished she hadn't given her name.

A friend of mine, Kim Donner Collins, recalls that her mother had a unique way of reminding others of the perils of judging. When Kim said something catty about someone, she frequently heard this line from her mother's repertoire of sayings: "Kim Donner's been born, but she hasn't died yet." Her meaning: Your life's not over; don't judge others lest you find yourself doing the same thing.

But no matter how many times we are confronted with reminders about judging others, it can be a difficult lesson to learn.

My husband and I were strolling along from shop to shop one Saturday afternoon in Sausalito when we decided to stop for an ice-cream cone and a restroom break. The only toilets nearby looked like those found in roadside parks. Not exactly the Taj Mahal, but serviceable.

I rounded the outer wall to see the typical line, which extended all the way out the restroom door. But the pit stop was no matter of choice, so I took my place in line and gradually made my way inside. Two feet, three feet, four feet ahead. Finally, I was even with the first stall door and could see the entire row of stalls lining the wall.

A burly man of about forty burst out of the last stall. Startled, the entire row of women pulled back as he made his way hurriedly past us and out the door. It looked like a scene from a movie where a hit man being chased by the cops pushes past people in a crowded hallway.

"What's *he* doing in here?" I remarked to the woman behind me. Several other women gasped and wondered aloud how long he'd been hiding in the stall. No one seemed to have seen him come in or noticed his feet under the stall partition only a few inches from the floor.

My first thought was that he had tried to attack someone. But wouldn't we have heard a cry for help from the stall? After a few seconds, I decided to give him the benefit of the doubt. He'd probably ushered a young daughter into the last stall and left her alone. The door was too close to the floor to see her tiny legs. But then, couldn't he have escorted her as far as the outside door and waited there? Or perhaps asked some woman waiting in line to watch out for her? Not a very good excuse to enter the ladies' restroom, I decided. Especially when it was so isolated from the other buildings.

I watched the closed stall door on the far end. No daughter ever came out.

Finally the second to the last stall door opened. It was my turn. As I walked into the stall, I caught a brief glimpse into the next stall—an elderly woman was seated on the toilet.

When I exited the restroom, I saw the man waiting on the park bench outside. His face was tired, embarrassed, sad. Beside him was an empty wheelchair that I hadn't noticed on my way in.

❧ ❧ ❧

You can't clear your own fields while you're counting the rocks on your neighbor's farm.

—*Joan Welsh*

Man does not live by words alone, despite the fact that sometimes he has to eat them.

—*Adlai Stevenson*

Get rid of all bitterness, rage and anger, brawling and slander, along with every form of malice.

—*Ephesians 4:31*

Words that Mold

WORK ETHIC OR WORRY ETHIC?

*H*urry, hurry, hurry. Wait, wait, wait. Work, work, work. The pace we keep as adults is often programmed when we are children.

A few years ago, we hired a young administrative assistant in our office whose reputation preceded her. Let me explain. When we have an opening or are about to add a position in our organization, we ask our other employees if they have candidates among friends or family members who might be interested.

Our office administrator piped up, "Yes, in fact, I do. From my other job. Rachel Lane is her name. She's very young, but quite mature. Dependable. Articulate. Good with people. Organized. Intelligent. And what I've noticed most about her is that she seems to have a strong work ethic. She doesn't waste time. If there are no customers in the store, she's straightening stock or whatever."

Sounded like our kind of person, I thought, and I suggested that our office administrator have her come in for an interview. Two days later, we made her a job offer on the spot.

Into her third year with us, the adjectives describing Rachel haven't changed. She's moved up to manager of sales and marketing administration and handles those responsibilities superbly. Our training workshop and speech clients depend on her to handle their scheduling without a hitch. Our suppliers trust her judgment on projects she supervises with them. Her colleagues depend on her for meeting her project deadlines. Her supervisors know that she'll work late if that is what it takes to get the job done right and on time.

When I commented on her excellent work ethic, she gave her mother the credit: "It's so funny to me as an adult which phrases come back to me in my daily life—things that my mother said over and over to me as a child. I've told her, and she seems calmly gratified that her words still come back to guide me. Somehow, I seem more surprised about it than she is, but then I guess that was her point.

"She always quoted that Bible verse to me: 'Whatever your hand finds to do, do it with all your might.' There are no unimportant jobs, she told me. Every job is a reflection of who I am and what I'm on earth to accomplish. And my mother always modeled, as well as told me, that I can do anything. Unfortunately, she stated that belief, 'I can do it, so I'm sure you can too.' Somehow this statement reassures and intimidates at the same time.

"But her impact on my work ethic is what stands out most in my mind. She always had two sayings: 'Never put off until tomorrow what you can do today,' and 'I'll worry about that tomorrow.'

"One of those statements almost always applies to any situation—I just have to decide which it is."

∽ ∽ ∽

I might not know how to use thirty-four words where three would do, but that doesn't mean I don't know what I'm talking about.

—*Ruth Shays*

Children seldom misquote you. They more often repeat word for word what you shouldn't have said.

—*Mae Maloo*

Words that Dispel Fear

OREO CAKE AND AMAZING GRACE

*L*eanne Daniels watched as five of her six young charges splashed themselves and each other in the swimming pool in the middle of nowhere. Never taking her lifeguard duties lightly, she settled back into her perch high above the pool to take in a wider view. She surveyed the surface to count bobbing heads once more and then scanned the crowd again for the only little girl who had not yet emerged from the cabin—eight-year-old Kimberly.

"Hey, Swiss Miss, look at me. Watch this," various swimmers called to Leanne. She smiled at them. All the camp leaders used nicknames for the week, and it was hard to decide who had the most fun with the tradition—the kids or the camp directors. "Swiss Miss, over here—watch me do a flip!" another called to her from the diving board. "Hey, Swiss Miss, time me—see how fast I can go," the oldest of the six girls demanded.

This was the most satisfying week of the summer. Pine Cove Encampment called it Scholarship-Free week. During this last week, disadvantaged kids from foster homes or orphanages got to attend without registration fees. And they came—all races, all faiths, all family configurations. They all had one thing in common—a difficult start on life. Leanne thought of the Tolstoy quote her senior English teacher had discussed with the class: "All happy families are alike, but each unhappy family is unhappy in its own way."

As she saw Kimberly finally come out of the cabin, she remembered the previous afternoon when the six girls had been assigned to her cabin and care. A little small for her age but full of life, Kimberly had caught her attention because she had arrived at the camp with her clothes and a blanket in a trash bag.

"Where do I unpack?" "Where's the bathroom?" "When do we play softball?" "How late can we stay up?" Kimberly and the rest had asked the usual questions, but the group this particular week had a few unusual questions like, "Do I get my own bed?" and "Do we get breakfast, and lunch, and dinner?" "Is it free?" "Are there prizes if we win the games?" For most, this was their first experience of camp of any kind.

"Swiss Miss, do we get to eat this cake every night?" Kimberly had asked Leanne after tasting her first Oreo cake in the dining room. Leanne had confirmed that dessert was indeed on the menu every night of the week. Kimberly had then asked every girl in the cabin for her leftover dessert.

Leanne smiled to herself, remembering how much Oreo cake one tiny little girl could put away. She climbed off her perch as Kimberly walked toward the play area and then edged off to the side of the pool.

"Ready to get in?" Leanne called to her. "You have to pass the lifeguard test before you can get in the water."

"I don't want to get in," Kimberly said.

"Why not?"

"I just don't. I can't swim."

"Well, you don't have to swim—"

"No, I don't want to get in." Kimberly started to pull away as Leanne draped a friendly arm around her shoulder. "No, really, I don't want to get in."

"But all the other girls are playing. It'll be fun," Leanne coaxed.

"No, I'll just watch."

"Hmm." Leanne backed away, "Are you sure?"

Kimberly nodded her head and sat down on the nearby bench, her expression drooped for the first time since she'd arrived on the campground. Puzzled, Leanne gave up and climbed back to her lifeguard perch to watch the other splashing campers. Several called to Kimberly to join them. But she could not be persuaded.

Leanne reconsidered the situation. Maybe the little girl wasn't as well-adjusted as she had first seemed. She'd told Leanne the first night that she was living in a foster home with three other children. Surely she would have had a little exposure to the give-and-take there around the dinner table, right? Leanne shrugged. Although loud as they splashed, raced, and pounded one another in the pool, the girls seemed to be a congenial group, grateful for the opportunity to be there.

But despite the invitations from the other girls to join them, Kimberly still refused to get in. Instead she sat alone on the bench with a forlorn look for the entire hour.

Later that evening in the worship service, Leanne stood with her girls. She noticed Kimberly had pulled away from the others before the speaker had begun and was quietly whimpering to herself. Leanne edged her way down the aisle toward the eight-year-old.

She slipped her arm around the little girl. "Kimberly, what's the matter? You were having such a good time yesterday. Did something happen?"

Kimberly shook her head and sobbed a little more openly. "Can you tell me what's the matter? Are you homesick?" The eight-year-old shook her head.

"Then what's the matter. If you tell me about it, maybe I can help."

The little girl mumbled, "I'm . . . I'm afraid of the water."

"Oh, . . . well, that's okay. A lot of people are afraid of the water. I'll help you learn to swim tomorrow."

"No, I can't. I'm too scared."

"There's nothing to be afraid of. Really. You just have to get used to it."

"But I can't help it." The little girl hesitated, as if not sure whether she should divulge the last part of her secret.

"What is it that scares you? It's not that deep. You could play in the shallow part."

Kimberly's face twisted into a somber, pained expression. She kept her eyes cast toward the floor, as she mumbled, "I'm . . . I'm afraid of the water because . . . because . . . because . . . when I was four . . . my mother . . . my *real* mother . . . tried to drown me."

Leanne felt herself swallow hard. All her months of training had not prepared her for this. Never before had she held a trembling little girl who'd made such a confession. She felt a physical ache in the pit of her stomach. What to say? What scars she must have. How could she ever hope to be near water again?

She heard herself say the words that represented her lifelong habit. "Well, . . . then we'll just have to pray to ask Jesus to take that fear away." She hugged the sobbing little girl to her and began to pray aloud softly.

At the conclusion of her prayer, Kimberly stopped crying. She leaned quietly against Swiss Miss for the remainder of the service. Afterward, she brightened and promised that she'd come to the pool the following afternoon at recreation time.

At the appointed hour, Kimberly appeared in her swimsuit at the bottom of the lifeguard stand. Leanne crawled down, took her hand, and helped her step into the shallow end.

But Kimberly clung to the side of the pool with one hand. She was in—but not free. Leanne got into the water beside her, "Okay, tell you what—I'm going to take both of your hands and pull you around. I promise I won't let go."

"Please, please, hold tight." And thus began each day's swimming experience. On the first attempt, Leanne got her to remove one hand from the side. After a few moments, Kimberly relented and gave Leanne both hands. She relaxed enough that Leanne could drag her a little farther from the side. "Amazing grace, how sweet the sound," the little girl started singing at the top of her lungs. The faster Leanne pulled her, the louder she sang.

She stopped singing suddenly and whispered conspiratorially to Leanne. "If I sing, I don't think about the water as much." Then she resumed her half-shout, half-song. They turned this way and that, slow and fast, but it was always "Amazing Grace" that came out. Each day, Leanne prayed with her that Jesus would take away the fear and then proceeded to pull her farther from the sides of the pool. On the fourth day, Kimberly permitted Leanne to turn her hands loose out in the center. On the fifth day, she was splashing the other little girls and playfully being splashed—all the while singing "Amazing Grace."

On day seven, she showed up at the lifeguard stand and announced, "I want to snorkel."

"Are you sure?" Leanne probed her determination, pride mingled with amazement. Kimberly glanced toward her playmates already in the other corner of the pool with the snorkel instructor.

"You have to put your whole head under—and your face

too," Leanne added, to make certain she understood. "Are you sure you want to do that?"

"I'm sure," her pigtails bobbed up and down. "Where's the gear?"

Leanne walked her over to join the class in progress.

A week after the camp ended and Leanne had returned to her fall semester of classes, she came home one evening to find an unexpected message on her recorder. When she recognized Kimberly's voice, she recalled giving all six girls in her cabin her personal number. It was not a camp have-to, but she had wanted to remain accessible to these girls as they returned to their "normal" lives.

The voice on the recording said simply, "Swiss Miss, I just wanted you to know that I gave my heart to Jesus while I was snorkeling. That's how I did it." There was a giggle. "Bye."

☙ ☙ ☙

Words are the most powerful drug used by mankind.

—*Rudyard Kipling*

Words that Enlighten

*D*uring a recent study group on a series called "A Woman of Noble Character," the discussion evolved around the many choices women have today in our society.

Elisa Gonzales listened intently. She valued her master's degree in counseling, which she applied liberally to raising her two-year-old. She had what she considered the perfect arrangement for her personal and family goals, a three-day-a-week position as a child development specialist, where she could take along her daughter and care for her during the day. But given the reality that this ideal arrangement would change when another child came along, she listened with intense interest as the discussion developed around her.

Some women in the group expressed satisfaction with their lives as working moms. They talked of the quality time they spent with their children. They talked of the positive qualities their children had gained in learning to accept more responsibility for themselves and their sense of teamwork as a family. They shared the pride their children seemed to feel in them as working moms who also participated in their "kid stuff." They talked of happy marriages in which both they and their husbands felt an additional link in sharing work-place problems and issues. They talked of their sense of accomplishment in the workplace and the opportunities to continue to learn and grow as individuals. They talked of their sense of calling to share their faith with coworkers in a world that badly needs a Christian influence. They expressed joy at their increased financial opportunity to support chari-table causes and ministries.

Others expressed satisfaction with their lives as stay-at-home moms. They talked of the opportunities they had to "be there" for their children around the clock. They loved being home at midafternoon when their children burst into the house to share an "A" on the difficult test. They talked of being home to comfort their kids when they had the sniffles and wanted hot chocolate and hugs rather than gym and geometry. They talked about the satisfaction of running the household and related errands so that their husbands could get ahead in their careers and still relax in the evenings and spend time with the kids. They talked about their sense of sig-nificance in their contributions to the school and community through volunteering for various charities.

Elisa listened to both sides. So what to do when the next baby comes along?

"I'm confused. So what do I teach my daughter?" she heard herself direct a question to the study leader. "I don't want to limit her choices. I want her to feel free about the opportunities women have today for an education and busi-ness success. Yet I also want her to feel free to stay home if that's what she feels is right for her and her family . . .

"What I'm getting at . . ." she paused long enough to see many heads bobbing along as if they shared the same puzzle-ment, "is that I don't want to *limit* my daughter. Nor do I want to *push* her into something she doesn't want. So just what do I tell her about her role as a woman, wife, and mother?"

The study leader summed up her guidance this way: "Don't focus on *limiting* or *pushing*. Neither word captures the real essence of what it means to grow up as a woman in today's world. Instead, focus on teaching her *the honor, the special privileges,* and *the special responsibilities* she has as a woman, wife, and mother. *Those* are worth your attention and time."

❧ ❧ ❧

How do I know what I think until I hear what I say?

—*Oscar Wilde*

May the words of my mouth and the meditation of my heart be pleasing in your sight, O Lord, my Rock and my Redeemer.

—*Psalm 19:14*

Words that Punish

Nothing prepares you for the day the man you love walks out the door into another woman's arms. There had been the telltale signs that women learn to recognize and interpret. The latest was an unfamiliar phone number written on a scrap of paper on top of the dresser.

Adrianna stood frozen with the telephone receiver in her hand. A little girl's voice answered on the other end of the line. "Hello?"

"Is Judd there?"

"Who's calling, please?" The little girl sounded like a precocious six- or seven-year-old, Adrianna thought.

"This is . . . Judd's wife," she said into the receiver.

The phone made a thud in Adrianna's ear as the little girl dropped it. Then she heard her yell in the background, "Mommy, there's somebody on the phone. She says she's Judd wife . . . I thought you said Judd was going to be *our* daddy!"

Adrianna dropped the receiver back into the cradle. Her arms and legs felt heavy, as if she were moving in slow motion toward the couch. When she finally reached the other side of the room, her life rippled across her mind's screen as if she were watching a videotape.

Number five in sixteen years. Over. Just like the others. After her first husband had died in a car crash at the age of twenty-six, she had not bothered to marry the others. Why should she put forth the effort, invest time and dreams, save money as if they would have a future together? No man could love her. No matter how much she gave, and gave, and gave. No matter what condition she found them, she had always set about to improve their lives. She brought them home and sobered them up or nursed them through a stay at some drug rehabilitation center. Having no kids of her own, she'd loved their kids and parents and brothers and sisters, opened her bank account to them, let them move in, introduced them to her friends and coworkers as the "new love."

All to have it come to nothing. Well, her mother had been right after all—she could never make a man happy.

Hadn't she killed her own father? That conversation eighteen years earlier still rang in her ears. Sitting on the couch with the room spinning around her, she could still hear her mother's voice. They'd been arguing about her decision to take a new job across the country, in South Carolina, a job that would require her to travel frequently.

"You're just taking that job to spite me, aren't you?" her mother had accused. "Just when I need you here. You're following some man, I bet. Aren't you?"

"Why do you do that to me—make me feel guilty?" Adrianna had pressed. "It'll be fun, a change, new people."

"Well, you could use new friends and fun," her mother had responded sarcastically. "The ones you've got here aren't worth having."

Adrianna had thrown down her hairbrush and had run outside, toward the back fence—as far away as she could get at the moment. Her mother had followed her outside, slamming the back door behind her. "You're still acting like you were sixteen. When are you going to grow up?! It wasn't enough that you had to drop out of school and shame the whole family!"

"Shut up, just shut up," Adrianna had yelled back. "Look who's talking. You—"

Her mother had grabbed her shoulder and spun her around. "You killed your father. Did you know that? You killed your father. He'd never have had a heart attack if he hadn't worried himself sick over you. You killed him just as sure as if you'd put a gun to his heart."

Adrianna sat on the sofa, limp. Her whole body felt clammy. She suddenly became aware of a tight rubber band around her forehead. What time was it? She looked out the windows behind her into nothingness. It had become dark around her, but there was no point in turning on the lights. He was gone.

❦ ❦ ❦

There are worse words than cuss words, there are words that hurt.

—*Tillie Olsen*

Words that Sabotage

Liz was glad to have the opportunity to have the men out of the house for a few hours. It was her first chance for a heart-to-heart talk with her future mother-in-law, Deborah. Although she and Todd had been dating for two years, she and his mother had never had extended time together without someone coming or going, asking for dinner, or taking them to a movie.

With soft drinks in hand, they both traipsed out to the patio to enjoy the cool afternoon breeze.

"So tell me how the wedding plans are coming," her mother-in-law-to-be said.

"Pretty good, so far. I never knew there was so much to it."

Deborah laughed and nodded understanding. "Oh, yes, I remember. I remember well. And if I ever remarry, we're going to take a cruise to Hawaii and marry at high sea."

"You've got that figured out."

"Now all I need is to meet a groom."

It was Liz's turn to smile. She genuinely liked her future mother-in-law. After all, she was the mother of the most handsome, fun, smart, kind man in the world. Obviously, she'd done a few things right along the way.

"You know, our families and our backgrounds—Todd's and mine—are a lot alike." She paused, then, "I don't know how much Todd has told you about my family."

"Not a lot. On the other hand, considering how stingy men are with details, he probably thinks I know you very well."

They both smiled and nodded in agreement. Liz continued, "Well, we have a lot of the same things in our past. Like—and I'm sure Todd has told you this—our fathers were both alcoholics. And Todd and I were the same age when our fathers left."

Deborah raised eyebrows as if that fact were news. "Todd and I never talk about his father anymore. I think we were just so relieved to have a normal life again, one where we could plan for an entire day without worrying about what we'd find when we came home."

Liz let that comment alone. She didn't want to stir up those memories from her own life. The unexpected disappearances. The late-night trips to some bar somewhere to pick him up. The screaming and the yelling. The blaming and the lying to everybody about where he was and wasn't and why.

"You know, I feel very, very blessed that Todd and I found each other," she said. "We're both so confident that God brought us together. It's just, well, amazing. It's like He divinely made us specifically for each other."

Deborah looked at her, without saying anything.

"My mother has told me that she prayed, even before I was born, that God would give me the right spouse. And she said that even when I was just a little girl, she prayed for my future husband. For his salvation, for his character, for his life's decisions."

Liz stopped. She hadn't meant to turn so serious. But it felt right to learn to share on a deeper level with someone she hoped to come to love dearly for a lifetime.

So she continued, "I believe that God knew in His infinite wisdom that we were perfect for each other and arranged for us to meet. I mean, think of the similar experiences we've had. Our emotional scars and baggage from the situations with our fathers. Because of all that, we're more understanding of each other. More accepting. More . . . well, everything."

Liz stopped again; she felt as if she were gushing.

Her mother-in-law-to-be still sat expressionless. Was Liz becoming too personal? Too philosophical for a Saturday afternoon? She added, "Well, I didn't mean to get so serious— I hope you don't mind. But it's just amazing how it has all come together for us. To realize God had a special plan for us and to just watch it all happen."

Deborah set her glass down and looked directly at her son's fiancée. "I disagree."

Liz waited.

"I don't necessarily believe that God has just one potential partner for us for a lifetime."

Liz reconsidered. Yes, her mother-in-law-to-be was a believer. But they'd never discussed their faith before. She turned Deborah's last statement over in her mind. She could understand her perspective. They divorced after Todd's father deserted her. And obviously, from her earlier comment, she hoped to remarry someday. Maybe God did have a "Plan B" as she'd heard others call it. The idea was not foreign to her. All she knew at the moment was that she felt strongly God had brought her and Todd together and that their relationship was meant to last for eternity.

But why press the issue? She and her future mother-in-law certainly lacked the depth in their relationship to debate something so sensitive and personal to both of them. She decided to drop the subject.

"No," Deborah said into the air after a moment, as if talking to no one in particular. "I definitely don't believe that in this world there is only one man for one woman."

Okay, Liz reasoned. Let it lie. She could deal with disagreement. Certainly, not everyone in the world had to agree with her personal beliefs. No matter what her future mother-in-law believed, it would not change her own confident feeling about the marriage. Let it alone. Hear her out and let the matter drop.

"I think God in his wisdom knew that we'd mess things up," her future mother-in-law continued as if thinking aloud. "So we have several potential mates out there." Deborah looked at Liz directly. "I believe Todd could be happy with any number of women. Take Pamela, for example, his former girlfriend. Lovely girl. Have you met her? Ambitious. Intelligent. Beautiful. I believe she and Todd could be very happy together."

Liz had no reply.

Many, many years have passed since that conversation. But even today, in her mother-in-law's presence, she always feels, well, interchangeable.

❀ ❀ ❀

Don't confuse being stimulating with being blunt.
—*Barbara Walters*

The difference between a prejudice and conviction is that you can explain a conviction without getting angry.

—*Unknown*

Words that Pray

THE WIDE-EYED SON

"*L*ance shot himself an hour ago." The voice on the other end of the phone was hysterical, but Sherry Clay recognized it as one of her two dearest friends.

"Where are you?"

"Home."

"I'll be right there."

As she flung on her clothes, swirled to turn off the oven and lights, and ran for the car, she tried not to think. At twenty-seven, Lance was still one of her "babies." She felt as though she'd raised him right along with her own four.

She tried to focus on the stripe down the center of the highway, but it was much too difficult. Why had they not known? The marriage, the birth of Keely, the divorce. It was all too much too soon.

But how could they have known? She thought back to the growing-up years. She, Lance's mother, Dickie Sue, and Priscilla had all been single at the same time, each raising children and trying to make a living alone. All three had worked together and become fast friends, sharing their children, their dreams, their difficulties, and their lives.

But why Lance? Reality kept hitting her in the face. He was always the jovial, entertaining, out-of-one-thing-into-three kind of kid.

Sherry stayed with her friend's family until the funeral home called to say they could view Lance's body. This was the moment they had all been dreading. He had shot himself in the mouth. The horror of what they might find when they saw him for the last time weighed heavily on Dickie Sue's mind.

Sherry, Priscilla, Dickie Sue, and her other son Brad crawled into the car together to head for the funeral home, leaving the other family and friends gathered at Dickie Sue's home. As soon as Priscilla backed out into the street, Lance's mom said, "Sherry, would you pray? I'm scared it's going to be so awful when we see him."

Sherry bowed her head, opened her mouth, and the words came, "Precious Father, today I know Lance is in your presence looking at you with wide-eyed wonder, just as he looked at all the other surprises in his life." The words continued to flow. When she looked up, there was a peace that had descended on those in the car that was beyond understanding.

A few minutes later, when they arrived at the funeral home, they were ushered into the room that held Lance's body. His mother walked in first, slowly. She peered into the casket and then called behind her, "It's okay, Brad. You can come on in. It's just Lance."

For days, as she talked to friends, neighbors, and family about the details of her son's suicide, Lance's mother mentioned the "wide-eyed" prayer that had given her such comfort on the most difficult day of her life.

❧ ❧ ❧

The flow of prayer is like the Gulf Stream, imparting warmth to all that is cold.

—Abraham Joshua Heschel

Words that Forgive

THE GIRL IN GREEN

When she applied for the job, Jennifer showed spunk. And the results of her employment tests underscored her intelligence. At the age of twenty-six, with a jaunt through Europe as a summer intern and a college degree under her belt, Jennifer went to work for a small law firm as a paralegal and newsletter editor. Her days were filled with challenging projects—from depositions to delivering subpoenas. She had the prerequisite budget, the approval authority to move mountains, and the fastest tools technology could provide to do her job with flair.

And she did. For the first few weeks. But it quickly became apparent that her personal problems had begun to overload her emotional circuits and cloud her attention to detail.

Almost daily, she received troubling phone calls from her father, from whom she had been estranged, and a dependent friend with too much time on her hands. Jennifer's nerves jangled at the surface. Her skin, typically as white as porcelain, grew red and blotchy. Whether from embarrassment, tears, or stress, she flushed from the top of her neckline to the tip of her forehead. No one had to guess when her emotions took control; the red rushed up her neck and face like a rising tide.

Life grew harder. Her mother's death at the age of forty-four from diabetes was still too fresh for words. Despite her disapproval, her father remarried, moved away, and dismissed Jennifer from his life. Her younger sister had boyfriend problems, and Jennifer became her surrogate mother. The troubling calls continued until one day Jennifer walked into her boss's office and asked for advice on dealing with her out-of-control life.

After lending Jennifer Christian books and a Bible from her personal library, the owner tried to talk with her about the love of a Heavenly Father. In the absence of her own earthly father, Jennifer could not fathom that certainty. She chose, instead, to pour herself into her work during the next few months and let the potential of earning more money motivate her to redouble her efforts on the job.

Bigger responsibilities called for an expensive, classy business suit, but she didn't have one. "Not a problem," the lawyer-owner of the firm insisted. "You can borrow one from me whenever you have an appointment with a client."

"Oh, I couldn't do that. I'll just save a little bit from each paycheck. I have a suit of my mother's that I can wear."

"No, really, I'm serious. Why don't you come by after work. You can try on clothes to your heart's content. Surely, you can find something you like in my closet."

Jennifer was obviously relieved and delighted. The job mandated that she have expensive clothes, but she was having difficulty paying the rent. She stopped by after work and fell in love with an emerald green suit. Her boss insisted that she take it and keep it at her house so she'd have it handy when she needed to see a client outside the office.

Jennifer's life seemed to brighten. She had new interests: grad school, a new love, and new friends.

Then one day, another employee walked into the owner's office, closed the door behind her, and announced some unsettling news. "Someone took some money—a hundred dollars—from our petty cash fund."

"How do you know?"

"I just counted it yesterday. There was a hundred-dollar bill and several small bills and a few coins. I hid the hundred-dollar bill in the center of the stack, thinking it would be safe until this morning when I made a deposit of the checks."

"Are you sure?" the owner resisted the thought.

"I'm sure. There's no mistake. I counted it. I *know* it was there."

Stunned and disappointed, the owner responded, "Well, someone else must have a key to get in here."

But she feared that was not possible. Feared, because she didn't want to believe that one of her trusted employees had taken the money. It wasn't the amount of the money; it was the violation of trust. It felt like a personal affront. Who would do such a thing?

An earlier scene flashed through the owner's mind. One night a few weeks earlier she had been in the building late when she had heard the front door to their office suite open. Quietly, she walked down the hallway toward the receptionist's desk and the front lobby.

Jennifer straightened up from the desk drawer. "Oh, . . . you startled me. I, uh, I . . . just came back to grab a book of stamps. . . . I, uh, I've got to mail this bill tonight. I'll go to the post office tomorrow and get another book to replace this one, okay?" The owner had nodded that evening and had gone back to work, relieved that it was only Jennifer back in the building. The scene now swam through her mind.

"I'm sure it's no mistake," the employee who discovered the missing money said again. "The janitors finished up before I left yesterday. On most days, I might not have noticed if anything had been missing, but I *know* there was a hundred-dollar bill in there. I just counted it yesterday. No one could have known about that money except . . . Jennifer."

"Did you ask Jennifer about it? Maybe she just borrowed it?"

"Well, I didn't exactly ask her. I just told her that I had discovered money missing. I gave her a chance to say that she'd borrowed it."

"And what did she say?"

"She didn't say anything. She just flushed from neck to forehead."

The owner knew the all-too-familiar giveaway.

A few days later Jennifer came in to resign "because she was making so many mistakes" and because she wanted to "think about things."

The owner never asked her about the money, but she continued to turn the situation over in her mind. Why had Jennifer taken the money? She would have given her anything in her closet. A raise, if that were necessary. Time with a counselor. Help in any way. But stealing? It felt like a slap in the face.

Two weeks later, on her last day of work, Jennifer walked in with a garment bag from the dry cleaners. "Before I leave—I know you think I've forgotten—I wanted to return this." She held the bag toward her boss. Tears welled up in her eyes, "I've really enjoyed wearing it. My friends say the color is exactly the color of my eyes. It has been my favorite outfit."

"Then take it with you."

"But . . ."

"I want you to have it."

She walked out with the green suit in one hand and the unread Bible in the other.

☙ ☙ ☙

You can preach a better sermon with your life than with your lips.

—*Oliver Goldsmith*

"But if you do not forgive, neither will your Father which is in heaven forgive your sins."

—*Mark 11:26*

Words that Lie

*P*eople often exaggerate to make a point. A friend of mine opened the lid to the toilet bowl in her bathroom to discover a swimming squirrel. Slamming the lid down, she called a pest control rep to the rescue. And it was amazing, she later acknowledged, how large that squirrel was when she first saw it and how small it was when the pest control representative actually pulled it out of the commode. Such exaggerations get laughs, make a point, hurt no one.

But in serious business settings, "exaggerations" turn into full-scale lies all too often. Sometimes with grave consequences.

Several years ago a partner and I walked out of a sales meeting with prospects from a Fortune 100 company who had been our client on training projects in the past. Our liaison with the company walked us back to the elevator, stepped inside with us, and then leaned the top of her head against the wall as we descended. I smiled, "Patti, don't tell me the meeting was that rough."

She turned around to face me, her expression grim. "It was all I could do to bite my tongue in there."

"What do you mean?" my partner probed.

"She's lying to you. Dorinne's lying. Out-and-out lying. I hate it. I don't know how much longer I can continue to work for someone like that." She then went on to explain that the senior manager had lied when she told us that the three other bidders had not quoted a fee for customizing. The truth was that the senior manager liked our work on past projects, hadn't even entertained the possibility of using anyone else for the work, and intended her comment only to force us to lower our bid.

The consequences? That company lost a good employee, Patti, who resigned because she didn't want to work for an unethical senior manager. And we caved in on the price because we couldn't tell a senior manager, "We know you're lying," without losing the client's business.

I wish I could say that was the last such incident in our nineteen years in business. But let me give you three other snippets of conversation. The first took place with a job applicant.

"Oh, I see here that you've worked for The Associates Corporation—that you were an editor there and wrote proposals," I observed as I surveyed the resume before me.

"Yes, I did." The blond, thirtyish applicant smiled broadly and confidently.

"Who did you work with there?" I asked.

"My direct supervisor was Antonio Sanchez."

"Oh, really? I know him. He attended a seminar I did out there some years ago."

The applicant smiled uneasily and reshuffled herself in the chair.

"So tell me a little about your newsletter—frequency? Editorial content?"

"Well, actually," she said, eyes darting this way and that, "I wasn't exactly *editor* of the newsletter. I, uh, proofread it. But they depended on me heavily for that."

"I see. And the sales proposals—you say here that you wrote those?"

"Well, again," she squirmed to realign her legs with the chair, "my boss was actually responsible for *writing* the proposals. I didn't actually *pull them together*—he did that. But I proofed them and pointed out inconsistencies."

I decided to probe a little further. "Now about the job before that. The salary you have listed for that job is quite high. Tell me a little about your responsibilities there."

She proceeded to overview her "management" position.

Then I said, "So how did you find that job?"

"Well, Mr. Carlisle respected my work at a previous job and hired me over when he moved to the new company."

"I see. So could you give me his phone number, please?"

I picked up my pen to write it down. She gave me a number.

Then she added, "Actually, he's a friend of the family. He said I could work there until I found something more in line with what I wanted to do. But, go ahead, and feel free to call him about my abilities."

"How long did you work for him?"

"Six weeks."

We ended the job interview.

The second conversational tidbit resulted from a job termination. The employee was dismissed for doing personal business on company time, sleeping at her desk, and making careless errors due to inattention to detail in her work. When she filed for unemployment benefits, the employee stated the reason for dismissal as "did not generate enough PR for the company." Fortunately, the state employment agency investigated the details of the situation and ruled against the employee who had lied, denying her claims to unemployment compensation.

The third situation involved Charlotte, a nurse, who inquired during a job interview whether she would be required to work weekends. She made it clear that she was looking for a position where she did not routinely have to work on Sundays. The director of nursing assured her that her schedule would require her to work only one in six weekends. Charlotte accepted the job under that condition. The first week she reported to work, she discovered that her schedule required her to work Sundays once a month. After the third week on the job, her work schedule was changed so that she had to work every other Sunday.

When she mentioned the issue, her colleagues laughed. "You must have been interviewed by Katherine. She lies about everything."

Lying happens in numerous ways: outright falsehoods, half-truths, omissions, and cover-ups. True—but incomplete— statements can also lead to false conclusions. Literal truth, when offered without complete explanation, can lead to literal lies. Knowing smiles accompanied by long silences can elicit wrong conclusions.

Intentions stand center stage. Ultimately, questionable intentions in communications cast doubt about character and culture—that of the speaker, those around the speaker, and the organization.

There are other ways to lie unintentionally—outdated data, opinions, and stereotypes. With our current information overload, data more than two or three years old can't support decisions or product designs. Correct, but outdated, statistics soon become incorrect. And even dangerous.

Ambiguity creeps in when we least expect it. Meanings depend on context, tone, timing, personal experience, and reference points.

Again, intentions control the tongue. A financial consultant related this situation to me about his firm: "We have two boilerplate formats for our reports to clients. When we go into banks and find several ways we can help them, we use the first format. That report gives our findings and a list of recommendations right up front.

"But if we go into a client organization and can't find much wrong—we don't have many recommendations for improvements and have charged them a big fee for the audit—then we use the second boilerplate report. We begin with background on our company, the credentials of our auditors, the various audit procedures used, and then we finally get around to the few findings and recommendations." He ended with, "But I don't think we fool anybody."

He's right. Purposeful gobbledygook only brings into question one's intentions. Lying in any of its forms—untruths, half-truths, omissions, exaggerations—destroys credibility that can never be regained.

✍ ✍ ✍

Lying is done with words and also with silence.
—*Adrienne Rich*

Think like a wise man but communicate in the language of the people.
—*William Butler Yeats*

Words that Disappoint

MATH MOUNTAINS

*H*eather waited until she got outside homeroom to look at the report card. Nonchalantly, as she slid her books into the locker, she pulled the card out of her backpack and opened it. Her eyes quickly scanned the first five periods. Then to math.

She let out a scream. "Hey, Lisa. Gerry. Alan. Wait up. I think I'll go with you after all. Aren't you headed for the Sonic?"

She caught up to her friends at the end of the hallway.

Gerry said, "Well, you're in a sudden good mood—McGivens didn't flunk you like he did half the class?"

"Nope. I did all right actually."

"So what's new." He goosed her in the ribs.

Later that evening, Heather breezed into the living room where her parents were already opening Lean Cuisines in front of the TV. Both looked up and spoke at the same time, "Hi, hon." Her mother added, "There's a leftover patty in the microwave. Help yourself."

"Sure thing. I'm gonna make a call first," she said. "Oh, by the way, here are my grades." She let the pink grade slip flutter to the coffee table in front of them as if it were no big deal and dashed off down the hallway.

As she reappeared ten minutes later and headed into the kitchen to warm the hamburger, she noticed their next-door neighbor had popped in. She waved to her through the doorway and retrieved the mustard from the refrigerator. Had her folks looked at the grade slip yet? You know your social life is in trouble when the big event of your day is showing your parents your grades. She smiled at the thought.

She slapped the hamburger patty between the buns and dug into the Doritos bag. When she came out of the pantry, she heard the next-door neighbor and her mother mention homework. Good, maybe her mother had looked at the grades. She pulled out the Sprite and reached into the cabinet for a glass.

"So I don't know what I'm going to do with him," the neighbor was saying. "He's doing his best; I know he is. But he still has trouble in biology."

"Oh, I know what you mean," her mother spoke now. "Heather's always had difficulty with math. She just can't get it. She does pretty well otherwise. But math gives her real trouble. She's just never been any good at it."

Her dad's voice added: "There are her grades—did you look at them yet?"

Her mother picked up the pink slip. Heather watched from the doorway. "See what I mean," her mother said to the neighbor. "A's and A+'s in everything but math."

"So what did she get in math?" her dad asked.

"Still an A-."

❧ ❧ ❧

A pat on the back, though only a few vertebrae removed from a kick in the pants, is miles ahead in results.

—*Royal Neighbor*

Correction does much, but encouragement does more.

—*Goethe*

Words that Comfort

GOING HOME

As they pulled into the used car lot, Granny Jordan told her eighteen-year-old grandson to pick out the car he wanted. It didn't take Vernon long to walk the lot and spot the green Chevrolet he wanted to test-drive. They took it for a spin, and as they returned to the lot, he gave her the thumbs-up. "This is it."

"Then just keep your mouth shut when we go back inside," she told him.

"Well, we don't know," she drawled to the salesman when the two of them sauntered back inside the lobby. "We'll think it over."

Vernon's mouth fell open. Think it over? What was this "think it over" line? This was *the car*. Hadn't she heard him? But he knew his Granny Jordan well enough to keep his mouth shut. She had not yet met her match in negotiating.

Two days later, Vernon came home from school to find the car parked in the driveway. "We finally got the price right," she offered with a twinkle.

Negotiating without the emotions—it was only one of the principles and techniques Granny Jordan taught the grandson who adored her. Whether it was negotiating with the realtor trying to buy her farm, persuading the visiting preacher to join them for Sunday lunch, insisting that her grown children live by the golden rule, or writing the president to veto the current tax bill, Granny Jordan communicated her mind.

So it wasn't exactly a surprise when she sat on the side of the hospital bed to talk to her grandson calling from Washington, D.C., the night before her knee surgery.

"Hey, Granny, you giving those doctors and nurses a hard time already?"

"They're doing okay by me—so far."

It was good to hear her chipper voice, Vernon thought as he teased her. Throughout his growing-up years, she'd taken primary responsibility in rearing him. So much so that she'd begun to call him Brother when she referred to him in front of the other family members. She'd been there for him during his parents' breakup. She'd been there for him at his sports events, sitting in the stands to watch every pass and tackle. She'd been there to send him off for his tour of duty in Vietnam. She'd been there to welcome him home. She'd been there to oversee his younger brother and sisters as they reared their families in the area. She'd baked his favorite biscuit breakfast every Thanksgiving Day.

It was good to hear her complain as she told him about the indignities of a stay in the hospital when people didn't always listen to old women who knew their minds. The world was right when Granny Jordan pronounced it so.

"Well, Granny, I'm sure you're going to be getting around much better by this time tomorrow night. Juanita told me the doctor said you could go home tomorrow or the next day."

"Brother, I'm not going home this time." She had suddenly turned serious.

"Yeah, Granny, you are. This is just a minor knee surgery. You remember—"

"No, Brother, listen to me. I'm not going home. I'm tired. Real tired. I just talked to Jesus last night and told Him how tired I was. He's gonna let me come on home."

"Granny, don't say—"

"No, Brother, it's okay. I'm ready. I just wanted to tell you myself so you could be prepared."

Vernon swallowed hard, told her he loved her one more time, hung up the phone, and walked into his boss's office to request time off to go home for his Granny's funeral.

"Well, Mama, the doctor said your knee's as good as new," Juanita reassured her mother when she arrived at the hospital the next morning to drive her home.

Granny just smiled.

"I'm going to go down and check you out. You know what the paperwork's always like. Marguerite will be here in a few minutes to help you get dressed, and then we'll get you down to the car to go home."

Half an hour later, Granny Jordan had a blood clot in her leg that quickly moved to her brain. She laid back on her hospital pillow and never regained consciousness. Two days later, she went home.

∽ ∽ ∽

God, it has been said, does not comfort us to make us comfortable, but to make us comforters. Lighthouses are built by ex-drowning sailors. Roads are widened by mangled motorists. Where nobody suffers, nobody cares.

—*W. T. Purkiser*

Words that Label

DO YOU KNOW JOE?

Neiman Marcus, an exclusive department store with several locations around the country, prides itself on offering something for everyone's pocketbook—from $89,000 sapphire earrings to $10 candies. And although shoppers can indeed find that range, the store's typical clientele more often *owns* hotels than works for them.

So it's no surprise that the merchandising managers and store managers have a difficult time impressing on their store associates the importance of greeting and servicing *every* customer—not just the well-dressed.

In fact, many department stores across the country have gone to great effort to make the principle of acknowledging every customer sink into each salesperson's psyche. Radio Shack, in particular, has a hidden camera in one of its stores to photograph shoppers. Then the managers select various photographs, along with the total dollar of that customer's subsequent purchase, to show new trainees how attitudes and words—or the lack of them—can affect their sales and profits.

Despite such training efforts about limiting perceptions, stereotypes remain in almost all industries, locations, and firms.

But the store manager at one particular Neiman's location finally had an opportunity to make her point with her sales associates.

One particular afternoon, a burly red-headed man walked into the store in a hurry. His hands and nails were dirty, his hair somewhat ruffled, his beard a little dark and scruffy. Then he paused in the aisle, glanced around the store, and waited as if expecting someone to approach him.

No one did.

The store manager in the back of the store noted the man's uniform and the lettering across his chest: "Joe's Heating and Air Conditioning." The man was carrying a duffel bag that hung awkwardly at his side. She presumed it was his work tools, but she hadn't even heard from anyone that they had called about an air-conditioning problem.

Since no one had approached the man to offer assistance or point him to the problem, the manager walked over and extended her hand. "What can I help you with, sir?"

"Hi, I'm Joe."

Without another word, he followed her to her desk in the middle of the Ladies' Fine Apparel. There he opened the duffel bag and showed her its contents—$60,000, to be exact. "I want to buy my wife a sable coat. That's what she wants, and I love her."

❧ ❧ ❧

A snob is anyone who looks down on us for a quite different reason than we look down on somebody else.

—*Sydney Harris*

An opinion is usually a prejudice with a few unrelated facts.

—*Unknown*

Don't air your prejudices—smother them.

—*Unknown*

Words that Inspire

GO, GIRL

The last class of my old professor's life took place once a week in his house, by a window in the study where he could watch a small hibiscus plant shed its pink leaves. The class met on Tuesdays. It began after breakfast. The subject was The Meaning of Life. It was taught from experience.

No grades were given, but there were oral exams each week. You were expected to respond to questions, and you were expected to pose questions of your own. You were also required to perform physical tasks now and then, such as lifting the professor's head to a comfortable spot on the pillow or placing his glasses on the bridge of his nose. Kissing him good-bye earned you extra credit.

No books were required, yet many topics were covered, including love, work, community, family, aging, forgiveness, and, finally, death. The lecture was brief, only a few words.

A funeral was held in lieu of graduation.

Although no final exam was given, you were expected

to produce one long paper on what was learned. That paper is presented here.

The last class of my old professor's life had only one student.

I was the student.

*T*hese paragraphs begin the bestselling *Tuesdays with Morrie* by Mitch Albom. Albom continues with his reflection of a favorite professor, whose influence changed his life. As I listened to Mitch at a writers' conference in Maui not too long ago, he told story after story of Professor Morrie Schwartz and his unique way of looking at the world. Listening to Mitch as he talked, there was no way one could miss the inspiration he drew from his professor's last breath and all the words that came before.

Gail Devers, three-time Olympic gold medalist, recalls the inspiration Olympian Florence Griffith Joyner gave her. Here's what she wrote in Joyner's eulogy published in *Time*, October 5, 1998: "When you think of Florence Griffith Joyner, you think of beauty, style, long fingernails and speed. But she was so much more. I first met Florence in 1984 and was captivated not only by her beauty but also by the beauty of her grace and the patience of her character. In 1996 at the Olympic Games in Atlanta, Florence came to my room before the 100-m final to give me words of encouragement. 'All right, Gail,' she said, 'go make history.'"

And Gail did.

Then there's the story of Terry Waite. From the early to the mid-1980s, Terry Waite, acting as a personal representative of the Archbishop of Canterbury, negotiated the release of Western hostages in Tehran, Libya, and Beirut, Lebanon. In January of 1987, on a mission to win release of the remaining U.S. hostages in Lebanon, Terry was himself taken prisoner. He was thrown into solitary confinement for four years, and then held for another year in the company of three other prisoners: Terry Anderson, John McCarthy, and Tom Sutherland. All told, Waite's imprisonment lasted 1,763 days.

In his autobiography *Taken on Trust,* he tells of the meaning of one single letter in his emotional struggle. One day, a guard opened his cell door and tossed in a card. It was addressed simply to Terry Waite, c/o Hezbullah, Beirut, Lebanon.

A woman had simply written: "People everywhere are praying for you and working for your release."

"That one card," he said, "kept me going for another two years."

For the majority of us, our words affect small numbers on a small scale. Yet that doesn't lessen their impact to those within hearing.

As a twelve-year-old, I sat in a youth meeting listening to Udine Slover. She and her husband, David, attended Baylor University, and her husband served as music director at our church on weekends. A beautiful brunette with Pepsodent-white teeth and a smile that filled the room, she could have won the Miss America pageant hands-down, had she chosen to enter. Instead, there she sat, pouring her life into our small town, population of 122, including five twelve-year-old girls, who hung on her every word.

At that age, the line that got my attention was this: "You can be popular," she assured us, "and never, never, never compromise your faith and your convictions." She should know, I thought to myself that Sunday morning. Her promise carried me through my teen and college years.

❦ ❦ ❦

A word aptly spoken is like apples of gold in settings of silver.

—*Proverbs 25:11*

Words that Accept

I'D LIKE YOU TO MEET MY WIFE

*T*here are few moments more pregnant with emotion than when we bring that special person home to meet the rest of the family.

After Vernon and I had been dating about eighteen months, we drove from Houston to Dallas to visit my folks. When we arrived in town, we learned my dad had had his second heart attack, so we went straight to the hospital. After we visited briefly, the nurses sent us home for the night, explaining that he couldn't have visitors until the next morning at 5:00.

That evening my mother looked weary. "Why don't you two women sleep in?" Vernon encouraged. "I'll get up and go to the hospital to visit your dad at five."

"But why?" I asked him. Vernon had gone with me to visit my parents several times during our dating, but they certainly hadn't established a close friendship at this point. I said, "Five o'clock is early. You're right that Mother needs to sleep, but I can go by myself."

He outargued me, so I gave up and stayed in bed the next morning when I heard him make his way out of the house.

Two days later, I got an engagement ring under the Christmas tree. At that point in our holiday trip, we were visiting with Vernon's family. The phone rang at their house shortly after I'd opened the ring and said yes.

It was my dad, calling from the hospital. "So were you surprised?"

"About the ring?"

"Yeah. Were you surprised?"

"How did *you* know?"

"Vernon told me. Two days ago. When he came up to the hospital to ask me if I had any objections."

I was floored. Fifty years ago that wouldn't have been a strange act; today it is. What made it even more unusual was that this was a second marriage for us both, and we were old enough to marry without anyone's permission!

I regained my composure and said into the phone, "So what did you tell him?"

My dad laughed. "I told him that you were smart enough and old enough to make up your own mind. But it was nice that he asked anyway."

Later when I questioned my husband-to-be, he explained simply, "We had a good visit. In my first marriage, I never felt that my wife's family accepted me. I didn't like that feeling."

That was the only explanation I ever got from him about that 5:00 A.M. visit.

But I have noticed that every time my husband starts to tell "our story," his introduction always starts like this: "Our years together have been great. Her parents, her kids, her whole family accepted me right from the start. They treat me like I'm one of them . . ."

The scene was the same with his family. I remember my apprehension on our first visit to his hometown. We took his mother and aunt out to dinner and to shop. His aunt caught both our arms for support as she stepped off the curb to get back into the car. She hugged both of us to her and said in her characteristically gravelly voice, "Well, Vernon, I sure do like your lady."

Her words felt like warm water on tight, sore muscles— relaxing, soothing, comforting.

Such is not always the case. An acquaintance of mine, the owner of a family business in which his three adult children have executive positions, has established an annual family ritual—a three-day retreat where he, his wife, and their three children discuss "family and business" issues—alone. The spouses of the children are expressly excluded. He justifies the retreat saying that their "frankness" at the get-together would make it uncomfortable for the in-laws and "some things" just weren't the business of the spouses.

A year later, he and his wife told me about their heartache in seeing their daughter, at the age of thirty-three, divorce her third husband. It occurs to me that the two situations may be related.

As a child I can remember hearing my grandmother say about my mother, her daughter-in-law, many times, "The Lord blessed me with two sons, but if I'd had a daughter, she couldn't have been better to me than Opal's been."

Why the recurring theme of acceptance *from* those we love *for* those we love?

It's not that we doubt our own decisions about whom we invite into our lives. But having others include them just adds another flavor to the swirled cone of joy mixed with affirmation.

One coworker explains it this way, "Education has always been very important in my family; both of my parents have master's degrees and have worked as educators. My mother would have chosen a very different kind of man for me than I chose for myself. She wanted someone very cerebral and intellectually stimulating for me—Mr. Boring. I wanted some-one smart, fun, and handsome, with common goals and interests. It meant so much to me when she told me that she wouldn't have chosen him for me, but that she could see I'd chosen the right person. Accepting him and making him part of our family has really been a gift from her to me."

From another: "I'll never forget what a wonderful feeling it gave me when my husband's grandmother introduced me to some of her friends. She said, 'I'd like you to meet my grand-daughter'!"

Words that accept new family members create a solid foundation for successful marriages. Words that reject start a hairline crack in the foundation that can eventually lead to collapse.

☙ ☙ ☙

One must know and recognize not merely the direct but the secret power of the word.

—*Knut Hamsun*

Do not let any unwholesome talk come out of your mouths, but only what is helpful for building others up according to their needs, that it may benefit those who listen.

—*Ephesians 4:29*

Words that Question

THE RULES IN OUR HOUSE

"Can I have some ice cream?" the four-year-old asked her grandmother.

"Sure, you can have ice cream at Gran's house. You want some now?"

The brunette curls bobbed up and down, and Gran went to the fridge to dish some chocolate ice cream for her only grandchild. The little girl finished it off rather quickly and then her interest turned to the windows.

"Can I go outside and play now?"

Gran again nodded. "Are you sure you want to go outside? It's pretty chilly today."

The curls bobbed again.

"Let's get your coat then. You may change your mind once we get out there. You're not over your cold completely. I'm not sure this is such a good idea."

"I'm not sick. See." She tilted her head back and turned her nose skyward.

"Well, no runny nose. You're right about that."

Gran retrieved their parkas from the hall closet, then followed her little charge outside. It was a blustery day. After a few pushes in the swing and a couple of circles around the patio, Whitney decided that she was ready for the indoors again.

"Can I build something?" Whitney asked once she got back to the warmth inside.

"Like what?"

"Like just something. Granddad builds. I want to hammer and saw something."

Gran shrugged her shoulders. Why not? If she knew Howard, the tools were probably still scattered in the garage. Luckily, the garage was attached and they didn't have to go back out in the wind. Gran shepherded Whitney through the connecting door into the garage. The four-year-old took a few licks with the hammer and laid it aside. The saw seemed more interesting. Afraid that the child might slice a finger, Gran stood carefully close with her arms wrapped around Whitney's shoulders, trying to hold the saw blade firm while the tiny hands pressed it against the wood.

When she couldn't press hard enough to make a cut, Whitney looked up at Gran. "Okay, it's all built . . ."

Gran raised her eyebrows.

"I'm just pretending," the four-year-old explained. "I'm just pretending it has doors and windows on it already."

They trooped back into the house.

"It's about time for your nap, isn't it?" Gran asked. After all, she'd been chasing her granddaughter around most of the day.

"But I don't want to take a nap."

"You don't want to take a nap? Your mommy said you always take a nap."

"But I'm not sleepy now."

"Don't you just want to try? To lie down for a few minutes to see if the sandman comes?"

Whitney shook her head and started to whine and pull
away from her grandmother's hug.

"Okay." Gran gave it up and decided they were in for a
long afternoon. What next? It took Whitney about two minutes to decide she wanted to color. Gran dragged out the coloring books and crayons. Whitney began to color the clowns
and the cows, the moons and the marigolds. Gran pulled out
a magazine and turned on the TV as she sat across the room
to keep an eye on her granddaughter.

"But I was watching that," Whitney said a few minutes
later, when her Gran started to change the TV channel.

"I thought you were coloring."

"I am. But I like to watch too."

"Well, I don't think this show is a good one for you to be
watching, do you?"

The four-year-old's head bobbed up and down again as
she chose another page to destroy with purple.

Gran left the TV on. Maybe the coloring would distract
her. The talk-show topic wasn't exactly one for little ears. But
then, how could a four-year-old pick up on the innuendoes?

After a moment, Whitney stopped her coloring and begin
to rub her eyes.

"Ready for your nap now?"

"No. I'm getting too big for a nap."

Gran managed to stifle a smile, and Whitney wandered
into the other room.

"Why don't you pick up all your toys while you're in
there, honey?"

"But I'm not through playing with them!" Whitney whined.

"Well, you could pick up some of them, couldn't you?

And put them back in the toy chest?"

"But I'm too tired. I don't want to."

Gran shrugged. No use talking. She'd seen her mother force Whitney to pick up the toys too many times through tears and tantrums.

Unloading the dishwasher, Gran soon felt her granddaughter underfoot again. What else could she do to entertain the child? Well, there was always a movie. Rent one? Or, maybe go out to a theater so they could eat M&M's without spilling them all over her floor?

Whitney started to climb onto the stool in front of the kitchen bar. The stool wobbled then rocked to a stop with Whitney safe on top.

Gran continued to put away the dishes, but she noted the pensive expression on the little girl's face. She sat there with her chin in hands, resting her stubby little elbows on the kitchen counter.

"I can do anything I want at your house," she said with a furrowed brow.

Gran nodded at her. Maybe she was having a good time after all. What a precious gift she was.

Then Whitney looked directly at her grandmother, chin still in hands, her eyes squinting. "You know what?"

"What?" Gran asked.

"Your house doesn't have any rules. . . . My house has lots of rules. . . . My mommy says the rules keep me safe."

∾ ∾ ∾

Don't be discouraged if your children reject your advice. Years later they will offer it to their own offspring.

—*Unknown*

Words that Scold

NOW LOOK WHAT YOU DID!

*A*s I write this chapter, I'm nestled into a quaint little inn in Toronto, Canada. I've just returned from a relaxing Sunday afternoon walk behind the inn and around the path that lines Lake Ontario. A myriad of other joggers, walkers, and bikers along the trail passed me by as the chilly breeze sent the yellow, red, and brown leaves drifting to the ground.

Two particular families caught my attention. About fifteen feet in front of me on the pathway I saw a little redhead, who looked about six or seven years old, skipping along beside her mother. A pigtailed brunette, who looked about the same age as the little girl in front of me, merged into the trail from my right. The second little one was accompanied by her mother and father pushing a baby stroller.

The brunette rushed across the trail, almost bumping into me in her dash to get to the water. Her mother said, "Megan, watch where you're going. You almost tripped that lady. And get back away from that water. Do you want to fall in?"

I turned and smiled in their direction, and the foursome fell into step behind me on the trail. At just about the same time, the redhead in front of me skipped closer to the water's edge.

Her mother said, "Peyton, why don't you let me walk between you and the water, and you can skip on the other side of the path. Would that work?" The redhead skipped over to the left side of the walkway.

Behind me: "Megan, stop that! Quit yelling and horsing around. You almost hit the stroller. You're going to wake up the baby."

Ahead of me: "Peyton, does that air feel cold on your throat? Why don't you try to keep your mouth closed so you don't breathe that air and get the sniffles." The little girl went from a lyrics to an off-key hum.

Behind me: "Get away from that dog, Megan. . . . Sorry, sir. . . . Don't you know not to pet strange dogs? They'll bite you."

Ahead, a moment later as the dog and master passed around me and caught up to the redhead and her mom: "Peyton, look at that dog. Isn't she beautiful? Give her room to pass."

Behind me: "Megan, stop it. Put those rocks down. Now look what you did! Look at the front of your jacket. You've got sand all down your front."

Ahead of me: "Here. Put my gloves on if you're going to throw rocks. They've got sand all over them."

I came to a fork in the path and decided to take the trail leading closer to the picnic tables and shade trees. My mind drifted back to a conversation I'd had on the previous Friday. A manager from a client firm had asked for an hour of consulting time, "to work out some personal conflicts" in her office she'd said when she scheduled the telephone appointment. On Friday, she overviewed for me several conflicts she had with her colleagues and staff at a new job, and I offered her suggestions to improve the situation.

As we wound up the conversation, she remarked, "You know, I thought I was leaving these problems when I left my previous job. But I guess I see that I just brought the problems with me. I know I have a very critical attitude, and it shows to my people. But that's the way I was raised—with two very negative parents. What do you do to get over it?"

Although I had offered her several suggestions for rebuilding relationships already turned sour at her new job, I had reservations that she'd be able to implement them without difficulty.

My dusty loop dead-ended back into the trail near the water. I regained my position between the same two little girls in our Sunday parade.

Behind me now: "Megan, you almost caught your foot in that bike. What are you doing? Pay attention to where you're going."

The biker whizzed past me.

Ahead of me: "Peyton, I hear another biker coming on our right."

I left the path around the lake and headed back inside the hotel. As I passed the wood-burning hearth in the lobby on the way back to my room, an odd thought struck me: What if either of these families invited me home for the evening to share a warm fire and meal?

Without actually being asked, I opted for Peyton's house.

❧   ❧   ❧

Children have more need of models than of critics.
                                                    —*Joseph Joubert*

Words that Uplift

WHERE DID I GO WRONG?

Barbara rolled over in bed to face the wall, so her husband couldn't hear her sniffling. The tears seemed like an every-night occurrence these days. She was sure he hurt as much as she did. But it just wasn't the same for men. They had their jobs to go to every day. They had schedules they had to keep. They had a purpose for waking up in the morning.

She felt his arm tighten around her, and she tried to fall into rhythm with his breathing. He slept soundly. She could not. For three nights, she'd tossed and turned until early morning. She'd finally fallen asleep only an hour or two before hearing the alarm jar her awake—to face the same issues.

Last night had been a culmination of sorts. Their middle son, Trevor, had left with his duffel bag to "move in" with his friend's family. Would he go ahead with the move? Would the friend's parents even let him stay? Would he drop out of school as he'd threatened? All she knew for certain was that he was angry, very angry, that she'd caught him and the friend smoking pot on the vacant lot down the street.

If it were only Trevor, she could look at things differently. Many families had a wayward child from time to time. She could blame it on his age—that terrible fifteenth year—or blame it on the influence of his latest friend, one who had just recently moved into the neighborhood.

But it wasn't just Trevor. Danielle, too, had decided that she was now too "sophisticated"—wasn't that the word she'd used last weekend?—to attend church with them when she came home for a visit. And against their wishes, she was considering moving in with her boyfriend. Yes, she could understand her twenty-year-old's need to find her own way at college. But her attitude had gone way beyond that. Yes, she was busy with a part-time job. Yes, college demanded study time. Yes, she had sorority obligations. All those reasons sounded good. But they just weren't the real reasons, she felt certain.

Barbara rolled over on her back, reshuffled the blankets, and stared at the ceiling. Where had she gone wrong? She'd had the kids in church since cradle roll. She'd attended every ball game, applauded at every school play, served as room mother more than her fair share, praised the grades as long as the kids did their best, got rained on during overnight camp outs. Why? Why, Lord? Why were they both so angry? Why had they relegated God to last place, if at all, in their lives?

She felt as though she were drowning. Instead of waking Robert with her shaking and sniveling, she swung her feet out of bed, pulled on her robe, and padded into the kitchen to pour herself another cup of coffee and wait for Sunday morning sunrise.

Five hours later, when she and Robert walked into the worship service, Barbara could imagine people talking behind her back, if not with blame, at least with pity. What did she expect? Trevor had been suspended twice in the last two months. The whole town knew it. But it wasn't just the embarrassment. It was the sense of failure. It was not knowing what to do next.

Just then a friend caught her eye. They'd not seen each other in a couple of years, since Stacy and her husband moved across the country. Stacy came toward her, and Barbara simply fell into her arms.

"The kids," was all she managed to get out. For once, no other words would come.

Her friend held her for a long moment and then whispered in her ear: "I know. And I know you're blaming yourself. But don't. I know a Father who has lots of rebellious children— and I can assure you it's not His fault!"

∾ ∾ ∾

Compassion is your pain in my heart.

—*Unknown*

Words that Laugh

ALL THE WAY TO THE TUB

My husband's Granny Jordan lived to be ninety without a broken bone. But that's not to say she didn't fall often. Whether she had an equilibrium problem or was just clumsy, the family never decided. Suffice it to say, she never hurt herself badly enough to decide to see a doctor for testing. And she never owned up to being clumsy.

It became a family joke when her teenagers left for school in the morning, "Now, Mama, don't go out to get the mail until we get home. We don't want you to fall off that curb—what would the neighbors say about finding you in the gutter?"

Later in life, she lived with her daughter and son-in-law. One night she got up to go to the bathroom, and when she stood up from the toilet bowl, she tipped herself over into the nearby bathtub. Not wanting to wake the "kids" at two o'clock in the morning, she just pulled a towel over her arms and lay there until their alarm clock went off.

When someone teased Granny Jordan about her falling antics, she'd laugh and explain, "I only fall enough to stay in shape."

❧ ❧ ❧

A cheerful heart is good medicine.
                              —*Proverbs 17:22*

The secret of being a bore is to tell everything.
                              —*Voltaire*

Words that Manipulate

KIDS NOWADAYS

Vera Rawlins peered through the screen door into the torrential rains. Again. What's an eighty-year-old to do for groceries? She hated paying the extra delivery charge for someone to drive four blocks with a couple of sacks. And besides that, she needed to make a doctor's appointment sometime this month. If it wasn't high blood pressure, it was the dosage on the allergy shots that needed to be adjusted. Doctors—they had a real racket going. And while she was out, she might as well have the cat groomed. Her nails needed to be clipped, and the bow around her neck smelled of sour milk and Cat Chow.

She pulled out the phone book and dialed to make the doctor's appointment. No hurry to go, but she might as well take something available next week and get it over with before she had to focus her attention on addressing Christmas cards. Her list had grown to sixty-eight friends. The closer the family member, the less likely they remained on her list. People these days were too selfish and busy to do what you needed them to do.

The receptionist on the other end answered. "Medical Towers. May I help you?"

"I need an appointment for my blood-pressure check," she said.

"Is this Mrs. Rawlins?"

"Yes, it is."

"I thought I recognized your voice."

"And I want the appointment next week."

"Well, let me see." There was a pause. "You're in luck. I've got something open Monday at 10:00, Thursday at 2:45, or Friday at 4:30. Which is best for you?"

"Monday. I'll take Monday."

She hung up and called her daughter at work. "Flo, I need you to take me to the doctor on Monday for my blood-pressure check. He may have to adjust my allergy medicine too." Vera never bothered with introductions anymore. Her children knew her voice, didn't they? After eighty years give or take a few, they should.

"Hello, Mother."

"Can you get here by 9:00? I need to take Puffy by the groomer's while we're out."

"I can't Monday. I'm going to be out in the field all day, and I can't take off work then."

"Fine. I'll walk."

"Mother, please. I've told you that I'm more than happy to take you to the doctor, or the vet, or the groomer's, or the grocery. But I just need a little notice."

"This is notice, isn't it? It's Friday."

"Longer notice than that. Could we make it later in the week? Then I could get someone to cover for me here."

"Never mind. I shouldn't have bothered you."

"Mother, please don't say that. You're not a bother. I'm happy to take you. It would just be easier for me if you could call me first and ask me what days I could be available, and *then* call for your appointment."

"I usually don't plan ahead to get sick."

"Are you sick? I thought it was for a checkup."

"I said never mind. I'll find a way. I'll get there. When you have kids who don't care, you get there anyway you can."

Vera hung up. Kids, you could never depend on them when you needed them.

❦ ❦ ❦

Show me one who boasts continually of his "openness," and I will show you one who conceals much.
—*Minna Thomas Antrim*

Language was invented so that man can hide the fact that he doesn't think at all.
—*Soren Kierkegaard*

Words that Trouble

DID YOU NOTICE YOUR ARM?

When fashion designer Gloria Pearson was a teenager, she and a friend were discussing new school clothes. Her friend turned to her and said, "I can't wear sandals—my feet are too ugly. But you can. You have beautiful feet." And from that day on, Gloria became aware and grateful for her feet.

But her daughter wasn't so lucky. "My daughter has big beautiful brown eyes—they're captivating. But someone in elementary school told her she had 'cow eyes.' And to this day, at age twenty-five, she still thinks she has terrible eyes."

People don't always intend to hurt with such comments. They're often simply insensitive to the effect their assessments can have.

I remember all too well my experience as a cheerleader in high school. The four of us girls met in July to choreograph and rehearse our new yells for the coming season. On one particular cheer, someone came up with the idea of having two of us move to the center, pick up the other two cheerleaders, and toss them into the air for the final flip.

"Good idea," sounded all around.

Then, "Okay, who picks up and who gets flipped?" someone asked.

We all shrugged, followed by a chorus of, "Doesn't matter to me."

Someone broke the stalemate. "Well, Dianna, you pick up, definitely. We're all lighter."

Humiliated, I accepted the assignment. At 115 I didn't feel all that huge, but they were correct. All three of them were tiny in comparison. To this day, no matter my weight and what the charts say, I think of myself as too heavy. "Lose ten pounds this year" has been on my New Year's resolutions list every year since I can remember.

Greta remembers overhearing a conversation between her mother and a woman in their church when she and her sister were preschool age. They both had long hair that flew in the wind as they ran and played. The woman, mother of three boys, commented to Greta's mother within the little girl's hearing, "If I had any daughters, I don't think I'd ever let them have long hair—it looks so witchy."

Tricia remembers a high school classmate, who offered her what he obviously considered a compliment: "You would be so fine—if you were just tan."

Then a year later, a boy at her church had a graduation pool party at his grandparents' house. When Tricia came out in her swimsuit, his grandmother yelled, "My gosh, you're so fair!" The woman forced her to sit under an umbrella with a towel around her shoulders.

Tricia explained how the sentiments about her fair complexion have continued through the years: "You wouldn't believe how many people, often complete strangers, have said to me, 'You need to get a tan.' In a time when everyone is supposed to be so color-blind, I can't understand why people feel it's appropriate to say something to me about an attribute I can't change—without risking my health."

And it's not just the vulnerable self-esteem of youth that such comments bruise. I heard one friend, at age seventy-three, comment after the last Christmas party season: "People keep commenting on my size. They say things like, 'You're not as big as a minute—what do *you* have to worry about with all these tempting desserts?' I can't help it; I'm small."

The comments seem senseless and endless:

"Your nose looks like a beak."

"Your hair looks like it's on fire."

"If your hips keep spreading, they're going to be bigger than your mouth."

"My gosh, you're tall—I bet you play basketball, don't you?"

"At this age, with hands on you the size of a basketball, what will you be when you get older?"

Gender, intentions, and real truth aside, such words can drastically affect self-esteem and trouble people for years.

We would all do well to adopt my friend Bob Murphey's attitude. A humorist from Nacodoches, Texas, Bob addresses audiences all across the country. In addition to his deadpan delivery and his Texas drawl, audiences quickly notice one other thing about Bob—his empty jacket sleeve pinned flat to the side of his suit. He lost an arm early in life. He tells his audiences about the time he ran into a smart-alecky young man on some back road during the course of business in his small town. The man kept staring and staring. Finally he asked a couple of leading questions, obviously meant to determine how Bob lost his arm.

When Bob answered each question without reference to the arm, the young man finally said to him rather bluntly, "Mister, . . . you don't have an arm."

To which Bob, in his deadpan voice and with solemn expression, responded, "Yeah, I noticed that."

✑ ✑ ✑

An honest opinion does the most good when sand-papered with tact.

—*Gloria Pitzer*

Most folks would benefit themselves and others if they would synchronize their tongues with their brains.

—*Unknown*

If you don't say anything, you won't be called upon to repeat it.

—*Calvin Coolidge*

Words that Reject

WITH FRIENDS LIKE THESE . . .

*R*ita rang up the sale, thanked the customer, and rehung the clothes left in the dressing room. As she returned to the service desk, several people waited impatiently for their purchases to be totaled, folded, and bagged. Management definitely didn't believe in overstaffing, even for the holidays. There was hardly time to do a job right and never time to do it over.

Rita scribbled a code for a refund in the wrong line; she realized it as soon as she'd done it. But the customer had already returned her charge card to her purse, six others were waiting behind her, and the floater had come to relieve Rita for a lunch break.

Handing the bag with the new sweater and receipt inside to the customer, Rita stepped back to let Jill up to the register to take the next customer.

"Thanks. I'm starved," she said to her replacement. "I'll see you in about an hour."

"Just a minute before you go," Jill pulled the merchant

copy of the receipt for the previous transaction from the register. "It looks like you did this form incorrectly."

"Yes," Rita quickly agreed. "I caught that myself just about the time I finished writing it all out."

"So aren't you going to redo it—correctly?" Jill persisted.

The customer that Rita had just finished serving stopped and waited with a harrumph, as if anticipating that the entire transaction would have to be done again.

"No, I didn't intend to redo it," Rita said. "It'll get the job done. The account number for the refund is on there—it's just in the wrong place. They'll find it."

"These need to be done correctly," Jill screwed her mouth to the side. "Carelessness causes all kind of grief if you work in Credit."

Rita bristled. Customers were witnessing the whole scene. Okay, so she'd made a mistake. It wasn't a big deal. The credit would still be given. If there was a problem, her employee number was written at the top. She'd redo the whole form later if necessary. What more did Jill want her to do—draw blood?

"Haven't you ever filled out one of these before?"

"Yes, Jill, I have . . ." Rita sucked in her breath. "I'll redo it if that's what you're wanting."

"Good. . . . I used to manage this department. I like things done right."

"Can it wait until after I come back from lunch?"

"I'd rather you do it now. I like to start off with the paperwork in order. I don't want to be blamed for other people's mistakes."

Rita bit her tongue, ducked her head, pulled out the refund book, and rewrote the entire transaction form. She could feel eyes of the surrounding customers staring at her. And certainly other associates had heard the whole scene. She wasn't a child, she thought. Her judgment about what was and wasn't acceptable was just as appropriate as Jill's.

Once the manager, not always the manager. Jill had moved on. That was one thing, Rita thought, to be glad about.

She finished the form, and as she left for lunch, she could see Jill still wagging her head and mumbling to the next customer in line.

As she sat in the cafeteria raking through her vegetables, she turned the conversation over in her mind. What had Jill been so upset about? Although they had never been bosom buddies, they'd certainly never had problems before at work. In fact, they had known each other for years, even before they had ended up working together. Their boys had played Little League ball together. They had served on PTA committees together. The last band fund-raiser came to mind; they'd spent hours loading boxes and boxes and boxes and boxes of chocolate-covered almonds into the band vans. Even in recent years, they'd compared notes on their kids' lives after they'd traded ball gloves for golf clubs during college.

Rita chewed on her roll slowly. What a silly thing to let something like this interrupt a friendship.

She returned to the service desk and Jill left the counter without a word. Resuming her place in the Christmas parade of purchases, she couldn't get the earlier interaction out of her mind. At midafternoon the situation kept gnawing at her. Occasionally, she'd catch a glimpse of Jill in the hosiery department across the floor. Both of them averted their glances.

No, this definitely should not be such a big deal, Rita reminded herself. Jill obviously must have something else bothering her. And, on reflection, maybe Rita had been too sensitive. So what if customers had overheard? They didn't know her from Adam—or Eve. Whatever. It was silly to spend the rest of the day stewing over a silly little conversation.

So as the crowd thinned out, Rita decided to make her way over to where Jill was rearranging the hosiery packages.

Walking up behind her, Rita said, "Jill, I want to talk to you a minute—to apologize about what happened earlier."

Jill faced her with a matter-of-fact expression and responded, "Well, I didn't mean to upset you. I was only trying to help keep things straight."

"I know. I know. It's okay. It doesn't matter. It'll be all right. We're friends, and we'll get over it." Rita smiled sincerely.

"No, no, no," Jill responded, with an icy glare. "We're not *friends;* we're *associates.*"

"Oh." Rita turned and walked back to her own register.

✍ ✍ ✍

We all need somebody to talk to. It would be good if we talked to each other—not just pitter-patter, but real talk. We shouldn't be so afraid, because most people really like this contact; that you show you are vulnerable makes them free to be vulnerable too. It's so much easier to be together when we drop our masks.

—*Liv Ullmann*

Tact is the ability to make a person see the lightning without letting him feel the bolt.

—*Unknown*

Words that Discourage

SURE YOU CAN'T

College professors wield great power with their erudite opinions. When I was returning to school, at the age of twenty-seven with two small children, to finish my master's degree, I enrolled in a creative writing class at night. As a part of our weekly assignment, we were required to bring our novel chapters, drama scripts, or poetry to read aloud and be critiqued by the other students and professor.

The last session, I stayed after class until my classmates had disappeared. Then I approached my professor as she cleared off her desk for the semester. "Excuse me, do you have a minute?"

She nodded for me to spit it out. I tried not to have puppy-dog eyes, but I respected her opinion immensely. After all, she was the only real writer I'd ever met; she had actually published a college textbook, which I held reverently in my hands.

"I was wondering if you could give me your personal opinion on my work this semester." I forged ahead so as not to leave a silence and risk a brush-off or casual dismissal. "I mean, it's . . . well, it's just that . . ." I stammered because I didn't want to telegraph to her the importance of her answer.

I started again, trying to muster a more matter-of-fact tone, "It's just that most of the people in class are not really serious about writing. It's a hobby. An elective. A pastime with them. But I'm dead serious—I've just quit my full-time job to write. And so I'd really appreciate your honest feedback about my work this semester."

I hugged my books and my latest manuscript tightly. It would take more courage than I could muster to ask her to read it. I wasn't fishing for a compliment, I reminded myself. I needed honest feedback. . . . No, the truth was that I wanted even more from her that evening. I wanted her to reaffirm the dream that I really could provide a living for my children by my writing efforts.

"Did you like Ms. Steinberg's stories?" she asked instead.

"Yes, yes, of course. They were excellent," I said, hoping she was about to make a comparison.

Instead, she rattled on about the obvious talents of the older Jewish woman in our class, who had read moving short stories to us every session about her experiences in Nazi Germany. I agreed with her assessment about the other woman's work. There was no doubt the woman's short stories pulled at my heart and kept the class spellbound.

But her talents had little to do with my dreams.

After staring at the floor for what seemed like ages, the professor finally glanced up at me, "Dianna, . . . novel writing isn't for everyone."

For a long moment, I couldn't speak.

I finally managed a, "Thank you for your time," as I backed out of the classroom and into the night.

I spent two years trying to prove her wrong. When my

first novel was published by a major New York publisher, I was tempted to send her a copy and say, "See there!"

Looking back on that moment, I've often wondered what my reaction would have been if she'd said: "Dianna, you know there's a lot more opportunity in writing nonfiction. I think that's where your real talent lies." I would have gone out of there humming, headed in the right career direction much sooner, with a clearer head and a more positive determination.

Ballooning dreams—you can either blow them up or puncture them. Inflating words can carry their passengers much further, longer, higher.

☞ ☞ ☞

"As a matter of fact" precedes many a statement that isn't.
                                        —*Mark Twain*

The heart of the righteous weighs its answers.
                                        —*Proverbs 15:28*

Words that Understand

BEFORE YOU SAY "I DO"

*D*ear Shannon,

I just wanted to drop you a note to say how sorry I am about your broken engagement. I know this is a very sad time for both you and Steve. But I'm confident that in your walk with the Lord, you certainly have learned that *no one* can tell you God's will for your life—but God. *You* are the person who needs to have that perfect peace about your decision, and if you don't, you have done the *right* thing.

I'm sure you know this, but I just wanted to reconfirm it in your mind: A broken engagement is far less traumatic and upsetting to all involved than a broken marriage. That's what engagements are for—making very, very sure. You've done that, and so your engagement period has accomplished its purpose—to be that last checkpoint before a lifetime commitment from which there is no turning back.

In helping you to ease the sadness and erase the doubt about the broken engagement, I wanted to share my own

122

experience with you: When I was engaged to Kenneth, I began to have a growing uneasiness that marriage was not the right thing for us. Although we were together only three weeks of our engagement period and then "finished" our engagement by long-distance while he was working overseas, I began to see (through our letters) more and more things that were troublesome.

But I swept them aside for several reasons: (1) He was a believer, and he told me he felt it was God's will for us to marry. (2) My parents had already spent money on the wedding plans that they could ill-afford to lose. (3) Didn't everybody have prewedding doubts? So mine were probably normal, right? Wrong.

For all these reasons and despite the growing knot in my stomach, I went ahead with the plans and lived through thirty-two years of deep unhappiness.

Your Uncle Ward, in his first marriage that lasted for three years while he was in his twenties, had the same doubts and even said he considered jumping out of the limousine on the way to the church!

Matt's experience was much the same. Your Uncle Ward and I had grave doubts during his engagement to Patrice and encouraged him to reconsider. He continued to have doubts as they broke it off and went back together numerous times. He decided to ignore those doubts, and it wasn't but a few months after their marriage that they were both aware they'd made a very big mistake.

All that to say this: I understand the sadness that you're going through. You feel bad for yourself, for Steve, and for your whole family. That's understandable. But try to dwell on the fact that God has the *perfect* person for you somewhere (notice that I didn't say "perfect person," but "perfect person for you"). He'll bring him into your life when the timing is right. Sometimes broken engagements are part of the process.

We love you,
Aunt Gail and Uncle Ward

❧ ❧ ❧

To profit from good advice requires more wisdom than to give it.

—*Unknown*

Advice is the only commodity on the market where the supply exceeds the demand.

—*Unknown*

Words that Warn

NOT MY BROTHER, HE ISN'T

"Look there. Under the truck. They're going to get him," Gary said as he moved his lawn chair farther away from his Ford pickup.

Melissa turned to her older brother. "What are you talking about?"

"Those men—under the truck."

Melissa glanced around the group to see if anyone else had heard him. Apparently, they had not. Her husband, two sons, and her mother were engaged in some backyard game, and the rest of the family were huddled in groups of two or three.

"Gary, come into the garage with me," she said. It was a command, not a request.

Her brother followed her. His jeans, with gaping holes, barely covered his legs as he walked. Melissa couldn't tell if he wore them out of need or by design. But his long, stringy hair looked no better. He smelled of sweat and axle grease.

"What are you on this time?"

"I don't know what you're talking about."

"Don't give me that—what are you on?"

"It's just speed. And you don't need to sound so high and mighty. Nadine doesn't care. She loves it when I'm on speed. I stay up all night and keep the house clean. And I run all her errands, so she can sleep in."

Melissa was determined not to get into another discussion about his and Nadine's lifestyle. His live-in girlfriend of several years wasn't exactly a credible judge of healthy living.

"You told Mother you weren't on anything anymore."

"Oh, come on. Get over it. What's the big deal?"

"She doesn't need to spend her life and her money having to take care of you."

Melissa's temperature rose several degrees when Gary's habits infringed on their mother. It happened all too often when she was in town visiting with the family; she could only imagine all the incidents to which she wasn't an eyewitness. The previous day's humiliation came to mind.

Gary had called her mother's house from the grocery store. "Come pick me up—I've got too many groceries to walk," he'd ordered.

Their mother had been in the middle of preparing lunch for the family, and so Melissa had done the duty. Gary's driver's license had been suspended again the last time he'd been stopped on a DUI. Although he lived only a mile or so from the store, he shopped by his own time clock, without thought for the inconvenience to his mother. He expected her to jump to his service whenever he needed a ride to or from somewhere.

He had tossed the bags of groceries in the trunk and crawled in beside her, muscle shirt flapping around his ribs as he started to roll a joint. "Don't smoke in my car, please."

"What's with you? Mom lets me."

"I'm not Mom, and I don't want you to smell up the car.

Surely, you can wait a mile." She had delivered him to his door with the groceries. No thank-yous. He had merely grumbled as he got out and headed into his house.

"What Mom doesn't know won't hurt her," he repeated now as he rolled a joint in the garage.

"You're hallucinating. You don't know what you're doing. You're killing yourself, and you're killing your kids."

"Speaking of kids, can you cut Brittany's hair? She needs a haircut bad."

"I'll be glad to cut her hair."

Melissa turned on her heel and left the garage. There was no use talking to him when he was high. She rejoined the rest of the family in the backyard.

Why? What had gone wrong with Gary? She had made a decent life for herself and her kids. Though not wealthy by anybody's standards, she and her husband had good jobs, she as a hair stylist and her husband with his own plumbing business. Her younger brother, too, had carved out a nice life for himself and was a responsible citizen.

Why did Gary refuse to accept the same responsibility for himself? For more than fifteen years he'd lived hand-to-mouth, on one kind of drug or another, living with this or that woman, moving in and out of their mother's life. He took her money and played on her sympathies.

But Melissa worried about his kids. What to do about them? Neighbors had reported Gary and his girlfriend for child neglect on several occasions, and still the authorities refused to remove the kids from his care. The eight-year-old was his; the two younger ones belonged to the live-in girlfriend.

Brittany sidled up beside her Aunt Melissa in the yard. Melissa gave her a quick squeeze and headed for the car to get the cape, brush, comb, and scissors that always traveled with her.

Brittany was a sweet child, loving and starved for attention. Melissa guessed that Brittany always hung on her when she visited because she was the only role model the child had in the family. At least she could give her a haircut. At least she could show her niece love and attention on these brief occasions when her brother brought the kids around the rest of the family.

Back from the car with the scissors, brush, comb, and cape, she took Britanny by the hand and began to search for a place to pull up a chair.

"How do you like school this year?" Melissa asked her.

"It's fun. I like it. I'm making good grades. But the kids tease me about flunking."

"Oh, don't you pay any attention to that, honey. I know a friend who stayed back in first grade just like you, but she graduated as an honor student in high school. You just keep studying hard. You'll do fine this year."

"I love you, Aunt Melissa. I really love you."

"And I love you, Britanny."

She bent down to hug her little niece's shoulders tighter. Then she noticed the white specks. White specks on every strand.

Livid, she sat the child down in the chair and said, "Wait right here for a moment."

Melissa went to find her brother for the second time that night. "Gary, come over here. I want to talk to you."

He sauntered over to where she stood under the tree away from the others. Anger bubbled just below the surface. He could live his own life, but not when it affected innocent children.

Somebody had to do something. She could feel the words boiling up and out like so much steam: "Brittany's got lice. I can't cut her hair."

"Yeah, we noticed. I've been working on that. So why can't you cut it?"

"Because it's highly contagious. I can't clean it off my scissors and cape. It'll spread to my customers."

"Okay," he shrugged. "So tell her you can't cut it."

"No. No, you listen to me for a change. I'm not going to destroy that little girl's self-esteem by telling her that her hair is too dirty for me to touch. I won't do that to her."

He stared, as if missing the point.

"I will *not* say that to her. Do you hear me? I won't do that to her." Her green eyes flashed; the words kept coming. "*You* are going to go over there and tell her that you don't have time to wait for her to get her hair cut today. And then you're going to the store to get what you need to get the lice out of her hair. And then you're going to change her bed sheets and wash her clothes and clean up that house. Do you hear me? You're going to learn to take care of those kids!"

Sometimes the best truth is the plain truth; the best talk, plain talk.

✑ ✑ ✑

No one objects to what you say that's worthwhile—
if you say it in a few words.

—Unknown

Formula for tact: Be brief, politely; be aggressive, smilingly; be emphatic, pleasantly; be positive, diplomatically; be right, graciously.

—Unknown

Words that Remember

RINGS, BEAUS, AND HORSES

"Come in here for a moment." Grammy motioned for Cheryl to join her in her bedroom closet, the inner sanctum to which few got invited.

Cheryl entered the closet and watched as her eighty-three-year-old grandmother reached into her jewelry box and turned around with two beautiful rings on the tips of her gnarled, arthritic fingers.

"I want you to have these rings."

Cheryl gasped. They were exquisite. One ring had three turquoise stones set in an elaborate eighteen-carat gold setting. The other was a luminous opal with a simple gold setting. Cheryl slipped them on. They fit perfectly on her slender eighteen-year-old fingers.

Her grandmother had married late in life, so Cheryl had known her only as an older woman. As she stood looking at the rings on her fingers, she was struck with how little she really knew about her grandmother.

She had observed the obviously loving relationship between her grandfather and her grandmother. They were devoted to

130

each other, rarely apart. Cheryl had watched the way Grampa patted Grammy's cheek with such tenderness saying, "That's my girl!" And Grammy always got the first bowl of popcorn when Grampa painstakingly made it each Sunday night. Cheryl could close her eyes and see her grandparents in their rocking chairs on the front porch of their big farmhouse, contentedly watching the sun set behind the Vermont mountains.

Now questions flooded her mind—questions about details of her grandmother's life she'd never thought to ask. Particularly the rings. She'd never seen her grandmother wear them.

"Grammy, they're beautiful. Where did you get them?"

"Oh, I had a few beaus in my day. A few who wanted to marry me."

Cheryl could hardly imagine her grandmother as a teenager, much less think of her as blushing fiancée or bride. She turned the rings from side to side to let them catch the light. Then she looked up at her grandmother.

"You never told me that you had other beaus who wanted to marry you," she said in a teasing tone, turning the word *beaus* over in her mind as she said it. It was an old-fashioned word. Even the sound of it made her wish she could have known what her grandmother's life was like back then.

"If you told all those other boys no, what made you decide to marry Grampa?"

Her grandmother smiled and said simply: "I saw the way your grandfather treated his horses."

✍ ✍ ✍

Kindness has influenced more people than eloquence.
—*Unknown*

People will overlook the faults of anyone who is kind.
—*Unknown*

Words that Limit

*F*ew people have more control over the self-esteem and potential success of young people than their parents and teachers. But the power of the tongue can also turn potential to poison somewhere in the process. And children remember for a lifetime.

On the first day of the fall semester, Mrs. Hamilton explained her selection process this way to high school students who had registered for her first-year Spanish class: "When I call your name from the roll, I want you to repeat after me. Then I'll make a judgment call about whether you stay in the class."

She began with the A's and worked her way toward the Z's. This annual ritual was no surprise. Upperclassmen warned those following them. To incoming students, it was momentary anxiety, nothing more. After all, they reasoned, it was a small school and teachers who taught electives ultimately had their fate decided by the popularity of their classes. No enrollments, no classes, no job. So it was with a sense of predestination that students rose to the test, yet they took their seats again with a sigh of relief. At least, this ritualistic exercise started them out in her good graces. Everyone so far had made it.

"Okay, we're to the R's. Rae stand up."

The lanky, sandy-headed boy stood up.

"Repeat after me: *'Buenas días, Juan. ¿Como está usted?'*" She waited.

He cleared his throat and with his best enunciation repeated: "*Buenas días, Guam. ¿Comb sta you-sted?*"

Mrs. Hamilton peered at him over the top of her glasses as she dropped her roster back onto her desk with a disgusted look. "You'll never speak a foreign language. Get out of here. Go find something else to take this hour."

She retrieved the list and moved to the S's as the embarrassed student collected his notebook and stumbled out of the room among the snickers of his classmates.

Less than ten years later when he found himself living in the border city of El Paso where a large population spoke Spanish and began to date a Hispanic woman, he would have found the second language more than useful.

Other students refused to let such harsh words and pronouncements from their teachers limit them.

Stephanie Sokolosky remembers wanting to be a journalist since her early teens. She loved writing leads, working to capture the who, what, why, where, and when all in one pithy paragraph. She loved interviewing people to scrounge their memories for just the right detail. But most of all, she loved the creative effort of turning hard, cold facts into intriguing stories.

But in Ms. Jerome's honors class, she struggled to write a paper that would earn her an A. No matter how much she looked for the perfect topic, no matter how much research she did, no matter how many times she proofread the paper for grammatical errors, her work still earned a C.

Finally, frustrated to the point of tears, she stayed after class to discuss the issue with her teacher. Maybe she could turn in a list of research topics and ask Ms. Jerome to help her select the best. Could she find better resources at the library than she had been using? Maybe there was a grammar book she should read? Whatever the problem, Ms. Jerome should know what to suggest to improve the situation.

So Stephanie asked, "What can I do to improve my writing and my grades in here?"

Her teacher responded: "You're a C writer and you'll never be anything but a C writer."

Stephanie left the room in despair.

Four years later, she graduated with a journalism degree from Arizona State's Walter Cronkite's School of Journalism. After working three years as a writer for news and talk shows at a major radio station and two television networks, she serves as director of marketing in the tax division at KPMG, one of the largest accounting firms in the country. There she writes marketing materials, public relations pieces, and proposals.

Some accomplishment for a C writer!

🖉 🖉 🖉

> She did not talk to people as if they were strange hard shells she had to crack open to get inside. She talked as if she were already in the shell. In their very shell.
>
> —*Marita Bonner*

Words that Affirm

LIFE IN THE MIDDLE LANE

*N*ine-year-old Mark stepped onto the driveway of his grandmother's house and then watched as the rest of his family piled out of the car. Why did Brantlee always get help? Why did Jay get more than his third of the seat? It wasn't that he wanted to be the "baby" of the family as his mom referred to Brantlee. But trading places with Jay wouldn't be so bad—he got to spend his allowance any way he wanted to.

Two years difference. Seven, nine, eleven. No big deal. So why should a measly eighteen months between them make such a big difference in how his mom and dad treated him?

But it did. If it was time to pick up a messy room, it fell to the two oldest—Jay and Mark, always Mark. If somebody got out of hard work, it was only the baby, Brantlee. If somebody got special privileges, it was always Jay, the oldest. If somebody "got away" with something, it was always Brantlee, the baby. He had come to think of himself as Mark in the Middle.

His dad waved the last child out of the car and locked the

door. Grandmother was in the process of hugging them all when Mark decided that he'd had enough.

"Dad, why do you do that?" he asked as they walked up the sidewalk together.

"Do what, son?"

"Why do you always say, 'Come on, Jay, Mark, Brantlee' or, 'It's time to eat—Brantlee, Mark, Jay' or, 'Stop that, Brantlee, Mark, Jay'? You always call my name in the middle. I'm always in the middle of everything!"

His dad just laughed, tousled his hair, and answered, "Stay out of the middle, then."

Mark jerked his shoulder away and sauntered into the house. He had asked a straight question. Why couldn't his dad just answer it? Why couldn't his dad understand how it was?

He slumped down onto the floor and watched as the rest of the family settled in for the visit. Mom wanted Grandmother's opinion on drapery fabric. Dad flipped the TV channels until he found the ball game. Jay sank into the big cushy pillow with a book. Brantlee tumbled outside to practice her cartwheels or whatever it was girls do.

Then his grandmother called him into the kitchen to see if she couldn't find the chocolate chip cookies. She handed him a cookie and said, "Mark, I heard you ask your dad that question outside, and I know the answer."

"You do?" Mark peered up at her through the wispy hair hanging over his forehead. At least Grandmother always loved him—no matter what.

"You know how you smear jelly between the two pieces of bread for a sandwich?"

Mark nodded, waiting with wide brown eyes.

"The reason you're always in the middle is that you're

like jelly in the sandwich. You make the whole family stick together."

"Hmmm," Mark said.

Ever since that conversation with his grandmother twenty years ago, he has been content with the arrangement. In fact, he and his brother now work together in their own business.

∞ ∞ ∞

Words are more powerful than perhaps anyone suspects, and once deeply engraved in a child's mind, they are not easily eradicated.

—*May Sarton*

Words that Accuse

INTERVIEWS AND INQUISITIONS

A woman approached me after hearing my session on gender communication differences, in which I'd mentioned that women ask questions to build rapport and men often resent them as traps. She laughed as she relayed her husband's earlier comment to her: "Honey, you don't *talk* to people; you *interview* them."

But sometimes, it's no laughing matter.

Our company designed a customer service training program a few years ago for a major airline. As part of that project, I'd written more than one hundred scripts illustrating poor customer service, which we'd shot in their studios. During preparation for a new speech, I remembered the earlier videos and one thirty-second vignette in particular that I thought would add a little humor to my speech. So I dialed the number that we had on file for that project, planning to ask for permission to use thirty seconds of the more than two hundred minutes shot.

The contact person we had worked with was gone. The new person in the job didn't know anything about the videotapes or training program but promised to find out about them and call me back with an answer about permission. I thanked her and hung up.

The following day she called to say, "I didn't know what you were talking about yesterday because I've never had anyone submit a 'permission' request. So I talked to our lawyer. She's here in the office with me and wants to talk to you directly."

"Fine," I said.

The lawyer never introduced herself, but the second voice sounded about twenty-five years old. She said, "I have the contract from the earlier project in hand. Can you tell me what you're asking us to do?"

Her tone was already agitated, I presumed, because my request might involve extra work on her part. That was understandable. But it couldn't require more than a two-paragraph letter of approval. I had handled many such requests myself from others wanting permission to quote something of mine. Here is the conversation that followed:

"I'm asking for permission to use a thirty-second excerpt from a videotape that I wrote and produced for your company several years ago. It was part of a much longer customer service program that I understand you no longer use. I'd like your permission to show that clip in a speech."

"So who has the videotape now?"

"Well, I have one copy in our archive files. Your office has the master and all other copies."

"So just how do I know you're supposed to have a copy in your possession?"

I was taken aback. "Well, . . . I don't know how you'd *know*. But the reason I have it is that your company liaison gave it to me."

"And can you tell me how I can *verify* what you're saying?"

"Well, you can ask any of the people from your company

who worked with me on the project." I pulled up the database and gave her eight names, including the president of her organization, who had been the primary sponsor of the program.

"None of those people are still here," she snapped.

"Well, I heard that you'd had a big turnover. Two or three of them called to say goodbye when they changed jobs. The project was finished six years ago."

"So you're saying that no one can verify the truth of what you're saying?"

"Look, I have no control over the fact that these people no longer work with your organization. I'm simply asking for permission to use an excerpt from the video. And I take it from your questions that you don't want to grant that permission."

"You're correct. I don't."

I was disappointed, but I decided to ask another question for the record. "Can you tell me if you're still using the program for training your staff? In our calls during the last few weeks as we tried to find the correct person about the permission issue, we were told that you no longer use the training video."

"Who did you talk with during those calls?"

I pulled up the database record and gave her six more names.

"What did they tell you?"

"They either told me they'd never heard of the program or that they'd heard of it but the company no longer used it to train staff."

"How do I know you didn't make an illegal copy and that you won't make one in the future?"

Stunned, I said, "I guess you'd know that by the very fact that I'm calling you directly to ask for *permission*. If I intended to use it illegally, it stands to reason that I wouldn't be calling you to alert you to that fact and ask for your permission."

"Do you have anything else of ours?"

"I have a complete copy of the training materials, if that's what you mean. They are the copies given to us by your organization when we completed the project. Your company president," and I called him by name, "specifically asked us to keep copies because he thought you might have to call on our trainers to deliver the program in cases of emergency."

The lawyer said nothing.

I continued, "You said earlier that you had the contract with you there now?"

"Yes."

"Then you'll notice on page four that we agreed on daily fees to do that. As I explained, that's why we have a copy in our office."

"Do you have the tape in your possession at the moment— can you put your hands on it?" she asked as if not hearing me.

"Yes, I'm holding it."

"Then I'm sending a courier within the hour to pick it up. And if you have anything else of ours, have that ready to give him also."

The conversation kept me awake two nights. And the unrest had nothing to do with permission to excerpt the video.

❧ ❧ ❧

Insults are the arguments employed by those who are in the wrong.

—*Rousseau*

The difference between a successful career and a mediocre one sometimes consists of leaving about four or five things a day unsaid.

—*Unknown*

One secret of successful conversation is learning to disagree without being disagreeable. It isn't what but *how* you speak that makes all the difference.

—*Jack Harrison Pollack*

Words that Advise

HOW TO MEET A MAN

*J*ason headed home to his apartment, feeling much older than his twenty-nine years. It had been a long week, a long year, a long life. No, not really so long, unless you considered your life span by the emotional trauma of what you've been through. On days like this, he felt like philosophizing; it helped him endure.

But it wasn't just the week. It was this tug of war about the future. Should he stay in or get out of the army? Yes, he was a dyed-in-the-wool patriot. He'd developed that patriotism early in his life from his community and his family. He lived in a country of choices—about school, about jobs, about friends, about a spouse.

And speaking of spouses, he thought as he pulled into the driveway in front of their house, newly furnished with furniture on credit. He saw the kitchen light on but no shadow across the curtain. Debi would still be upset. Another dinner in silence.

That's what complicated the whole decision. On the one hand, the military offered security, role models he'd never had in a father, travel around the world, and an advanced degree—if he could keep the grades up and the post commander happy.

On the other hand, Debi considered military life anything but an opportunity. It was security, but not success—at least not as her parents defined it. It was travel, but nothing romantic during hardship tours in out-of-the-way places like Bangladesh. It offered time and salary to earn a master's degree, but why put your life on hold for three years in exchange for mere tuition when your in-laws could simply write the same check? And why, she kept asking, would he just not accept the position her father offered in his company?

Her car was home. Dinner on the way. As Jason closed the front door behind him, he tossed his cap on the sofa and headed for the kitchen. Maybe a kiss would melt the tension between them—at least for an evening. He suddenly felt bone weary.

"Hi, little one. Have a good day? What's for dinner?"

She didn't answer him. She just stood looking at him.

He couldn't read her. What was going on? Was she still battling the military issue? Short on money again? Was there new furniture she wanted but thought they couldn't afford? Or maybe her parents were flying in, and she didn't want them visiting just yet—until he agreed to move back to their hometown and take the job offer? For the entire three years they'd been married, they'd been at odds—about everything. From fun to finances. Different goals. Different ideas about what was important in life. Why had he not noticed all these differences when they were dating?

Then he remembered the feeling of panic that had swept over him as the limousine picked them up and headed for the large Greek Orthodox wedding, a ceremony during which he never realized the exact moment the officiating minister had pronounced them married. The scene came back to him. The huge crowd of well-wishers, mostly friends of Debi's parents, the band, the dancing.

But mostly the panic. The panic that he had attributed to the conventional wisdom that all brides and grooms had second thoughts just before the "I dos." If he had it to do all over again, would he have the courage to say, "Let's wait. Let's slow down. Let's be sure. Let's don't do it at all"?

He refocused on the moment. She stood silhouetted in the kitchen doorway, her dark eyes focused on him. He thought she looked especially beautiful, petite, fragile.

What to do? Argue again? Avoid it at all cost? Offer to take her out to her favorite restaurant? Suggest she fly home to visit her folks for a change? Whatever would make her happy. Whatever would give him a little peace for a few days.

She cleared her throat and handed him a piece of paper. "Would you sign this?"

He unfolded the papers and simply stared. A divorce? Proposed settlement? Couldn't they talk it over? Why? How did she come to this?

"I've thought it over. I've talked to my parents and to a lawyer. I've made up my mind."

He swallowed hard and felt his jaws tighten. Steel. Stand tall. Square shoulders. Soldier. He could take it. He would handle it. He knew the look when he saw it.

"Yes, I'll sign it." The furniture to her, the bills to me. The car to her, the bills to me. The stereo to her, the bills to me. He scribbled his name without even reading the rest of it. Then he picked up his cap and backed out of the room, out of the house, out of her life.

Later that night, lying wide awake on the sofa at a friend's house, he stared at the ceiling.

He had to make the call. He had to make the call to the

one person he most dreaded to disappoint, the grandmother who had raised him. He had to be the one to tell her before she heard the news from an outsider.

He pulled himself up from the sofa and dialed her number. Once he got the words out that he and Debi were splitting up, his grandmother responded uncharacteristically about his bride. "I never felt good about Debi and you."

Now she told him? That was news to him. Debi had always been welcomed into the family, included in all their get-togethers, best friends with his sister. He held the phone.

She repeated, "I never felt good about you and Debi together. You didn't meet her in church. You didn't marry her in church. You never went to church together. . . . Always look for a wife in church. You have to have a spiritual bond."

In the wee hours of the morning, her words of assessment and advice played over and over in his mind. She had been right. His concern for the spiritual had been swept aside for his decision of the moment. Never again.

Those words became his action plan for finding the wife God intended for his life companion.

☞ ☞ ☞

When words are scarce they are seldom spent in vain.

—*Shakespeare*

The mouth of the righteous brings forth wisdom.

—*Proverbs 10:31*

Words that Bridge

The Charles de Gaulle airport in Paris looked huge. The Boris Pol Airport in Kiev, Ukraine, looked ominous, whether from the physical layout or from the bleak stories she'd heard of the country, eighteen-year-old Leanne Daniels couldn't decide. She gathered her two bags from Baggage Claim and worked her way outside toward a new world. It was the first time she'd flown anywhere outside the United States and the first time she'd been a part of something so exciting, yet so unsettling.

She looked to her left, then her right. Where to now? Standing outside in the brisk air, she pulled the scrap of paper with directions from her coat pocket. The directions were brief. A family was supposed to pick her up and drive her to the Kiev Bible League storehouse. Once there, she was supposed to wait on an outside bench for Vladimir, the husband of Renata, the camp director. Her home for the next six weeks was to be the Christian Camp for Kids in a village 100 miles south of Kiev.

Shortly, the designated family of doctor, wife, and four children pulled up to the curb. Like American children, the kids bounced out of their bus, pointed at the airport billboard advertising soda, and begged for a treat. If what her sponsors had told her was true, the family could hardly afford cabbage and potatoes, much less soda.

The father motioned for her to come toward them. What to do other than smile? Armed only with her pocket dictionary, Leanne tried to say "hello" in Russia. The family greeted her with hugs and hustled her into the car for the trek to the next relay station in this "run" for camp. She could do with about twelve hours of solid sleep. Shivering, she pulled her coat tighter around her, hoping it would get both easier and warmer.

After the two-hour drive, the family pulled over to the curb beside the Kiev Bible League. The small building looked deserted. She had been told it was the place where they stored Bibles to be distributed around the country. They let her out to wait for Vladimir, another benefactor of a warm car whom she'd never met. As she pulled her luggage out of the family's car and waved goodbye to them, she closed the door on the only "friends" she'd met on the trip so far.

But she was determined not to give in to exhaustion and fear. Both feelings periodically crept into her consciousness and threatened to overshadow her commitment. Having volunteered for the camp with no pay for the summer, she sometimes tottered between her determination to change lives and a wish to go back home to a warm bed, a loving family, and a "normal" summer with the rest of her high school friends as they prepared for their freshman year at college.

She sat down on the bench and waited. She felt like an actress in one of those spy thrillers. With her turned-up collar and alert eyes, she was sure she looked the part. People milled all around her, but no one spoke. At least not in English. She waited for Vladimir. How would he introduce himself? Would he recognize her from the photo? What if someone had made a mistake in the directions? What if no one ever came for her?

A Russian teenager approached the park bench and motioned toward the empty spot. She spoke Russian and she carried clothes in a brown paper bag. She seemed to be asking if she could share the bench. Leanne gestured for her to take a seat, and then yanked out her dictionary again to find the phrase to introduce herself.

The girl's name was Tonya. So far, so good, Leanne thought as she flipped through the pocket guide to find other phrases that might be helpful in striking up a conversation. The process seemed arduous but well worth the effort when Tonya's eyes lit up every now and then with a word recognized.

After a moment, Tonya's eyes grew wide, and she pointed to Leanne's power bracelet of black, red, white, green, and gold. The jewelry had been a great idea back in the United States, where the wearer hoped to initiate a conversation with someone who showed curiosity about its meaning. The colors represented the Gospel story. But what good was the bracelet going to do her in Russia, where she couldn't explain anything?

With a sudden big smile, Tonya pointed to the bracelet and blurted out in perfect English, "Do you love Jesus?"

"Yes! Yes! I love Jesus! That's why I'm here." Leanne's eyes filled. Finally, somebody understood something she could say. They both began to try to speak in their own language at the same time. After a few moments of further sign language and sharing of scraps of paper and tickets, they discovered that they were both headed for the same camp as sponsors.

Just then a man pulled up in front of the park bench and motioned for them to join him for the three-hour trek to the campground. As they climbed into the car with the man called Vladimir, Tonya became Leanne's caretaker, motioning for her to lean her head on her shoulder and rest from her flight.

Later at the campground Tonya became Leanne's interpreter for the first few weeks, pointing out the latrine as a *banya* and the swimming hole as a *playa*. Tonya had come from a family of eight children, and her parents had sent her to the camp to work for the summer because they couldn't afford to feed her.

Together at the camp, the newfound friends enjoyed a steady diet of borsch and full days of Bible study, crafts, and recreational activities with the children they'd come to love and teach. The Russian children showed their appreciation to the Americans at the camp with a very special gift several weeks into the summer—a toilet seat to place over the hole in the ground.

As the days of summer flew by, Leanne grew accustomed to the new culture and customs. But she never forgot the relief and peace of Tonya's first words, "Do you love Jesus?" that united them in purpose.

❧ ❧ ❧

We have to face the fact that either all of us are going to die together or we are going to learn to live together and if we are able to live together we have to talk.

—*Eleanor Roosevelt*

Words that Calm

I NEVER GOT THE CALL!

Standing beneath the Courtesy Vans sign at the St. Louis airport, I watched as the van driver hopped out and scurried toward my bags on the curb. "You Booher?"

"I am."

"Never got the call," he snarled at me. "Never got the call!"

I nodded at his explanation and crawled inside to the center seat as he threw my bags in the back of the van with a thud loud enough to be heard on the runway. I watched as he lumbered around to the driver's side and crawled behind the wheel.

"The d— dispatcher is the stupidest . . ." He finished the rest of the sentence under his breath.

He jerked the van back out into the traffic lane and sped off. Then he turned his attention again to me by way of the rearview mirror. "She said you called three times, but I never got the call. And then *I* get yelled at. *You* people yell at me, 'Where you been?' but I never get the call. And it's the skin off *my* nose, not theirs. I work for two hotels—they share me.

What a joke that is—they share me. And I'm on a run for one hotel, and then I get this call from the other hotel. So when I tell them it'll be twenty minutes, then they starting yelling at me. How the hell do they expect me to be two places at once? And you people are standing here screaming, 'Where is he? He was supposed to be here an hour ago!' And I get blamed. I get here and you people are fit to be tied, yelling at me. The dispatcher is too stupid to tell 'em I'll be there in twenty minutes. No, she tells them I'm on my way when she knows d— well I'm not. And then *I* get yelled at!"

He paused for the first time in the tirade.

I took opportunity to say, "I understand. That must be really frustrating."

"It is."

He fell silent. It wasn't that I felt so understanding, but rather that I was too tired to protest further. We drove along toward the hotel for another couple of minutes, his face straight ahead. Then he lifted his eyes to the rearview mirror again.

"So. Where you in from?"

"Dallas."

"Business or pleasure?"

"Business."

"So what do you do?"

"I speak at conventions and corporations. And write books."

"Oh, yeah? I once had a movie producer in my van." And he proceeded to tell me about the interesting fares he'd driven, about his two kids, about his wife, about his dreams for future education and his efforts to get his pilot's license.

Twenty minutes later we pulled into the hotel entrance. He whistled as he got out, retrieved my bags from the back, carried them all the way inside the hotel to the registration desk, and thanked me profusely for the tip. "You have a nice stay now and a safe trip back home."

As he hustled away, I wondered how many wars, divorces, or job terminations might be prevented if we more often responded, "I understand. That must be really frustrating."

❧ ❧ ❧

He who smiles rather than rages is always the stronger.
—Japanese proverb

Anger makes your mouth work faster than your mind.
—Unknown

Words that Support

PASSION AND PLANS

I climbed into the dogsled feeling more fear than excitement. It was not the dogs but the temperature that day in Anchorage that gave me cause for concern. After all, I'd have Mike standing on the back of the sled guiding us every foot of the way. He checked my boots, gloves, and parka once more. Finding things in order, he signaled the dogs and we were off.

Within seconds, it felt as though we were speeding along faster than a roller coaster. But we were gliding along at ground level with wind of -38 degrees hitting me in the face. I hadn't dared ask the chill factor. As we took the first corner, I leaned to the left to miss a tree limb on my right.

But I wasn't quite fast enough to maneuver upright again before a small twig caught me in the left eye. It began to water. Within seconds the tears froze among my eyelashes, and I could not completely open or shut my eye. I yelled up at Mike, standing straddled behind me on the sled. "Can I take off my glove? I got something in my eye."

"Sure. For a second or two. But get it back on quick."

I pulled my hand free of the glove and tried to wipe my

eyelashes and eyelid free of the frozen tears. It didn't work. Fearing frostbite on my hand, I gave it up and managed to pull my glove back on.

It was a long hour's ride.

When Mike and the other trainer and sled deposited my husband and me at the back door of the Noskos' house, they ran the dogs on down the hill to the pens. Vernon and I disappeared into the house where Mike's wife, Tracey, had hot chocolate ready in front of a roaring fire.

As she helped us strip out of the protective clothing and dry our jeans and shirts, dampened by melting snow that somehow had managed to slip inside all the layers, she asked how we'd enjoyed the trip.

But I was much more interested in *her* frame of mind. I'd just concluded a speaking engagement in Anchorage where a large majority of the group had complained about the surroundings. Most had referred to those who went back to the mainland for a vacation or business as being "outside." When I'd questioned the meaning of that phrase earlier in the week, someone had explained that it was the typical way of speaking of someone who had "escaped" back to the Lower 48.

But Mike's wife, Tracey, wore a relaxed, pleasant expression rather than the strained one I'd seen on too many faces the previous few days. So I asked her as we three huddled in front of the fire, our hands wrapped around the warm mugs, "So how did you two end up here?"

"Mike was in the army. They transferred him up here after boot camp. Then when he got out, he loved it so much that when they wanted to send him back, he said, 'No way.'"

"So you like it up here." It was a statement rather than a question.

"He likes it up here," I noticed her phrasing and omission. "He just fell in love with the huskies. He decided that was what he wanted to do. So he got out of the army and bought his own team."

"Does he race them?"

She nodded. "Last year was his first year to enter the Iditarod. He didn't do too bad—for his first time out." She continued with an explanation about their months of preparation, the unexpected difficulties during the race, how many dogs had actually finished the race, and their plans for the next race in the spring.

"So what do you two do for a living? This isn't full-time, is it?" I feared my ignorance was showing.

"You mean, how do we pay the bills?" she laughed at my embarrassment. "Well, I work at the post office. Mike—he has a job a week. Shoveling snow. Driving a school bus. Construction work. Whatever. Just as long as it doesn't interfere with his time to train the dogs. He's passionate about those dogs."

I nodded.

She downed the rest of her hot chocolate, glanced out the window at her husband with the dogs, and then added with a smile. "He'll win. I know him. He's passionate about anything he does. We'll win."

Somehow I believe her.

❧ ❧ ❧

Nothing is as useless as the right answer to the wrong question.

—*Unknown*

Most of us like people who come right out and say what they think—unless they disagree with us.

— *Grit*

Words that Blame

A STRONG WILL AND STRICKEN HEART

Finally finished with the bedtime battle, Katy turned out the light on her sleeping four-year-old and rejoined her grandmother in the kitchen. As she poured them both a cup of tea, Nanna asked her, "Honey, do you have to go through that kind of routine every night to get that child in bed?"

Katy shook her head. "Every night. Every single night." Her eyes filled with tears. "I try, Nanna. I try to make him mind me, but he's the strongest-willed little boy you'll ever find on God's green earth. I do time-outs, everything. What am I doing wrong?"

Nanna raised her eyebrows in playful fashion. "You could spank, beg, promise, or time-out all day long, but I don't think you're going to get through to him."

Nanna watched her twenty-two-year-old granddaughter add a little water to the already-weak tea. For a short moment, she wanted to reach out, hug her, and cry over her, not her adorable great grandchild, who was the current topic of conversation.

How hard life had become for her. She would do anything if she could erase all those poor decisions of an immature teen. Her thoughts raced as she watched her granddaughter add sugar and a slice of lemon to the tea. Both she and Katy's mother had held such high hopes for the girl's future. She had wanted Katy to finish high school, go to college, meet a nice young man, and make a storybook marriage. But all those dreams had been dashed when, in a period of rebellion during her junior year of high school, Katy had run away to marry a boyfriend of a few months. And all too suddenly, she had three small children underfoot, too little confidence under her belt, and rent that routinely came due too soon.

How she wanted to take Katy in her arms and rock her like she'd done so many times before she had children of her own.

Katy turned around to face her. "So what am I going to do with him, Nanna. I just can't control him. Josh isn't that way. I can tell him no and he stops what he's doing. But Brent just must have his way—about everything. And he can't live on goldfish, grapes, and graham crackers!"

Nanna understood her frustration. "Unfortunately, honey, when we pick their fathers, our kids don't just get the good traits. He is exactly like his father."

Katy looked as if she'd been slapped across the face.

The moment Nanna heard the words roll off her tongue, she wished she could recall them. It was no secret to Katy that the family hadn't welcomed her husband with open arms, but how could she have made such a callous remark?

Katy realized that her past decisions had made life harder for all of them. She had confided disappointment, and even despair, about her future prospects in life without a college education. Yet here she was, standing in the kitchen of the person she knew had always loved her more than life, asking advice on how to handle this strong-willed child, and hearing instead something so punishing! How could she not interpret the comment to mean that she wasn't very bright, that she had been a disappointment to the family, that her child was a mistake.

Katy turned her back and walked toward the window. She stood looking out into the darkness.

Nanna apologized. "That was a hurtful, senseless remark. That darling baby has picked up a few bad habits from me, as well as from the rest of the family. He isn't *just like* his father, or anybody, for that matter. I'm so sorry I said that."

Her granddaughter looked out the window for a long, long time before she regained her composure enough to pour her cold tea down the drain and take her sleeping child home for the long night.

☞ ☞ ☞

We cannot always control our thoughts, but we can control our words, and repetition impresses the subconscious, and we are then master of the situation.
—*Florence Scovel Shinn*

Words that Trust

DON'T LEAVE HOME WITHOUT IT

*T*he long line snaked around, like one for tickets to a rock concert in town for only one performance. The line had begun to form as early as 4:00 A.M. The draw was an opportunity to sign up for three personal fifteen-minute consultations with the agents and editors of choice at the fifth annual Maui Writers' Conference.

Maggie Bedrosian fell into line behind a particularly weary soul, a young bearded man who kept talking through his yawns. They quickly struck up a conversation and shared their life stories much like airline passengers do when they know they'll never see each other again upon arrival at their destination.

Finally, the bearded man reached the ticket desk at the head of the line. Eagerly, he pulled out his American Express card and handed it, along with the scrap of paper containing his choice of agents, to the woman behind the table.

She turned back to the man. "Sir, I'm sorry, but we don't take American Express."

"What?"

"Do you have another card we can swipe?" the woman asked, trying to be helpful.

"Oh no!" the bearded man said, clearly distressed. "How can you not take American Express?"

"Sir, there are other people waiting behind you. Do you have another card, cash, or a check?"

"No," his voice was low this time. He glanced back over his shoulder at the line that snaked about 100 yards behind him.

"You just don't understand—I've *got* to get these appointments. I've come all the way from North Carolina."

The clerk said, "Sir, would you step aside a moment so that—"

"Here, put it on mine," Maggie said from behind him, touching his elbow with her credit card.

He turned around and stared at her, "But you don't even know me!"

She smiled. "But I know what you've *been through*."

☞ ☞ ☞

The man who trusts people will make fewer mistakes than he who distrusts them.

—*Camillo Di Cavour*

Words that Clarify

WHY CELEBRATE TUESDAYS?

Sixteen-year-old Barry shuffled into the house after school on Tuesday afternoon to find the family room filled with balloons. He began to rack his brain. So what was the occasion? He ran through the family birthdays. Nope. Graduation. Who graduated on a Tuesday—in April? He slung his backpack on the sofa and headed out to the patio.

"What are you doing home from the office?" he called to his mother. "What's happening here?"

"Celebration," she called to him as she dusted off her hands and started back inside with some zinnias. "I came home early."

"Celebrating what this time?"

"Carrie got an A on her history test."

Barry smirked. "So are we hiring a band too?"

"Come on, help me. Can you set the table? She went by the library to drop off the reference books, and I want it to be ready by the time she gets here." She handed him a knife and two cucumbers. "You can slice those and toss them in that bowl there."

"Is this some biggie or something? Like she doesn't graduate if she can't get through Mr. Weingarten's history?"

"Barry, you know what a hard time she's had with history—forever. Last year too."

"So this is just your plain old everyday test we're talking here?"

"I don't know how much it counts, if that's what you're getting at. But it's the one I've quizzed her on for the last two days."

"Reckon it ever occurred to her to crack a book herself? Ouch!" He dropped the knife and pressed the flesh back into the newly wedged index finger.

"What did you do? Be careful. There are some Band-Aids in the drawer behind you. Is it bleeding?"

"It's fine." He wrapped a paper towel around it tourniquet style and kept chopping.

His mother finished filling the vase with zinnias and began to turn the pork chops. "If you're finished with that salad, would you go see if you can rouse your brother and tell him we'll be eating in about fifteen minutes. He's upstairs. And how was your football practice? I didn't hear you say if you thought you were ready for Friday's game."

"We're ready."

Barry clumped up the steps two at a time to find his younger brother. "Mom said dinner in fifteen minutes."

Pete answered without looking up, "Hey, come look at this. It's cool. You can order all this stuff on-line."

Barry punched his younger brother affectionately on the shoulder and disappeared into his room. Another day, another party. Well, at least his mom wasn't expecting them to dress up in costumes. She got the weirdest ideas sometimes for her instantaneous parties. Obviously, Carrie was going for some kind of record—see how many things you can fail at so you can get rewarded when you achieve at normal level. He remembered the celebration when she finally understood fractions. And the slumber party for about two hundred of her closest friends when she qualified for the volleyball team. Qualified, mind you, not *started*. She hadn't started a single game.

He sat down on the side of the bed to take off his shoes and socks. It was Pete who needed a few more parties, if anybody did. That kid had him worried. He sat in front of a computer or over a book from dawn to dusk.

Barry fluffed up the pillows and slid back onto his bed, flipping on his stereo. He recalled overhearing his dad and mother talking together after their trip to the principal's office for Pete's one and only school fight. He'd gotten into a fist-fight with another third-grader on the playground. According to his mother as she'd summed up the conversation to his grandfather later in the week, she had told the principal, "In a fight? Good. That's the first time he's ever stood up for himself."

Barry also remembered seeing Pete's annual from fifth grade. Someone had written in the back, "Too bad you're moving—I won't have anybody to beat up."

Poor kid. He hated to admit it to himself, but his little brother was the classic geek. That's who needed the friends and the party.

"Barry? Pete? Come on down for dinner," his mother called.

He scooted off the bed and headed downstairs. He didn't intend to let good pork chops go to waste—even if it was in Carrie's honor.

Carrie did the typical, "Oh, mom, this is great" routine before they sat down to dinner. Barry took it all in in reasonable fashion. Afterward Carrie disappeared into her room, and Pete back to his computer. Dad loaded the dishwasher and then joined him in the backyard to throw a few passes.

They wrapped up their practice half an hour later. "Son, you better whip their tail Friday night." His dad caught the ball, tucked it under his arm, and started inside.

"We will, Dad. Their tight end's out for the season. I'm predicting we'll beat 'em by twelve."

"I'll up that to eighteen," his dad said, following him inside. "I'm heading for the shower. How about giving your mother a hand with the balloons on the fan?"

After he and his mother had freed the fan, he flopped down on the kitchen counter.

When she noticed him standing behind her, she said, "What are you staring at me for?"

"I want to ask you something."

"So shoot. I'm all yours."

He had second thoughts for a moment, but then continued: "You always help Carrie. You're like her . . . cheerleader . . . or something—for everything. Even the simple, everyday stuff that everybody else does anyway."

"But Barry—"

"You do, Mom." He didn't want to sound like the jealous kid, but, well, it didn't make him feel all that good. "And you help Pete. You're always trying to cheer him on, to get him to make friends, to get him to take interest in things. You're just always helping them."

"And?"

"And you never help *me*, that's all. I just want to know, . . . why not?"

His mother looked at him, as if aware of the situation for the first time. But Barry knew she couldn't argue with him. Facts were facts, as he always said. His mother seemed to turn the observation over in her mind.

After a long minute, she said to him, "Well, . . . I guess . . . I've never helped you, . . . because you've never *needed* it."

Barry thought it over.

It made sense. Was that a bad thing—his self-sufficiency? He *did* feel good about his successes so far in life. He left the room that night, and he never concerned himself with the matter again.

❧ ❧ ❧

It is harder to ask a sensible question than to supply a sensible answer.

—*Persian Proverb*

Deafness has left me acutely aware of both the duplicity that language is capable of and the many expressions the body cannot hide.

—*Terry Galloway*

Words that Dare

STAND UP, SPEAK UP, MOVE ON

As she got closer to the animal in the middle of the crowded intersection in San'a, Yemen, Vicky Ulrich realized it was not an animal at all. A very handsome man, who looked about twenty, glanced her way. His face lit up with a beautiful smile as he darted furtively from side to side to avoid the cars hurrying past him in all directions.

"Please, money. Help me," he begged. A few tossed him ryal notes; most did not. After all, it was God's will that he wore rags and begged for his next meal. In the Arab culture, physical deformity was considered a punishment from God for the sins of one's father or one's own.

Vicky continued to stare through her car window, stricken with horror at his condition. He crawled around in the road in front of her on all fours. His feet were shriveled and limp. Filthy clothes hung limply around his body. Only occasionally did he dare glance up into someone's eyes as they handed him ryals and then passed on by.

Slowly in the traffic, her car edged closer toward him. The

irony of the scene struck her. Such a handsome, young face. Such a deplorable predicament.

Her car moved still closer, and she rolled down the window. "You need to walk like a man, not like a monkey. And you *can* do it. I'm going to take you to a therapist."

He glanced up at her, as if in disbelief that someone had directed comments to him specifically.

She grasped his hand through the car window. "You do want to walk, don't you? A doctor will get you crutches, and your legs will grow stronger."

He stared at her. Vicky couldn't tell if his expression was disbelief, anger, or puzzlement.

Then to appeal to his macho pride, she said, "You want to be a man, don't you? You aren't *afraid* to see a *woman* doctor, are you?"

In his eyes, she could see her own three sons of about the same age. Her tone softened. She nodded reassurance to her dare. "It's safe—I'll stay with you the whole time."

For a full year, Vicky drove the young man to a therapist. And even that decision had not been an easy one for the young Arab man. He had been taught it was a shame for a woman to see a man's body. Yet, Vicky had dared him, no, commanded him, to walk like a man, hadn't she?

The therapist worked with him on stretching, lifting, and bending exercises—all with the purpose of building his muscles for normal use.

Within three months, Mahmoud was fitted with a shoe for his right foot and crutches. His left foot remained too deformed to wear a shoe. But still the exercise sessions continued. Mahmoud worked hard.

With each upright step, his self-esteem blossomed. As he could physically look people in the eye, he could also metaphorically look people in the eye. More people began to see his beautiful smile. The next plan was to find him a job so that he could support himself.

The staff at the American Embassy, well acquainted with his former life, expressed amazement at how far he'd come through his rehabilitation efforts. They hired him as a guard, with a smart uniform to replace his rags.

On his new salary, he returned to his formal education. It would be hard to find anyone who would doubt that someday in the not-too-distant future he will be helping other street beggars.

❧ ❧ ❧

A voice is a human gift; it should be cherished and used. . . . Powerlessness and silence go together.

—*Margaret Atwood*

Words that Compliment

DIETS AND DREAMS

The mother opened a bag of chicken nuggets for her whining toddler seated in the shopping cart at Wal-Mart. I started to push my cart around hers in the aisle when she straightened up and faced me. The button on her lapel said, "I lost thirty-seven pounds."

"Excuse me," I said. "But I noticed your lapel button. You look great and so energetic with your son."

"I feel great," she beamed. Her disposition seemed sunny, and her manner with the crying toddler was patient.

"That's quite an accomplishment—thirty-seven pounds. I've been losing and gaining the same ten since eighth grade."

She laughed. "Yeah, that was me. I'd tried every diet in the books—grapefruit, garlic, high protein with low carbs, high carbs with low protein. You name it, and I've tried it. But I finally found something that works for me."

My passing comment turned into a full-scale conversation. "I guess you could say my son has a new mom now. I used to come in from work exhausted and grouchy. In fact,

I've quit work. I used to work just so I wouldn't stay home and eat all day. Now, food's not such a temptation. I feel like a nice person again. I'm in control."

She stopped and looked at me more intently. "How do you think this sweater looks on me? I just bought it. It's been years since I bought anything like this. And I've got a few more pounds to go."

I took in the multicolored burgundy weave. "You look very nice in that. The colors are great on you."

"I can do this," she said as she started to push her cart on down the aisle. And she wasn't talking about navigating her way through Wal-Mart.

∽ ∽ ∽

Some fellows pay a compliment like they expect a receipt.

—Kin Hubbard

Words that Criticize

NOW YOU DO, NOW YOU DON'T

My fourteen-month-old began to cry when I reached out to ease her into the arms of the nursery worker. "Mommy's gotta go to big church now."

She answered me with a louder wail.

"You remember Ms. Sparks, don't you?" I said, as the nursery worker gathered her into her pressed pink apron. The nursery worker tempted her with patty-cake, then a bar or two of "Twinkle Twinkle, Little Star," followed by promises of juice and crackers.

Nothing worked. With my three-year-old hanging onto my skirt, I tried to soothe the younger one with kisses and last-minute hugs.

"What's the matter with Lisa?" her brother, Jeff, wanted to know.

"She's tired, honey. She didn't get her nap this afternoon."

We were attracting a crowd now as other parents began to drop their kids off for the evening worship service. I began to feel eyes on me as I tried to comfort and then cajole my daughter from my neck.

"Looks like somebody's unhappy," someone called to me over her shoulder as she deposited her obviously well-adjusted kids in their respective rooms.

Then someone else, "It's really hard on little ones sometimes, isn't it? We have to be a little creative to get them to stay."

Then another: "Hi, what's wrong with Lisa—she looks unhappy."

"Lisa, don't you want to come inside and play with Mike?" someone else coaxed.

She shook her head and began to whimper louder.

"What's wrong with Lisa tonight—she sick?"

"She's just tired," I explained again for what seemed like the tenth time. Finally, Lisa turned loose of my shoulder, and I coaxed her into the classroom. Ms. Sparks stepped outside the nursery and into the hallway with me. "Bless her little heart. Sometimes I think, . . . well, I hope you don't mind me saying this, but you bring your kids to church too often."

I just looked at her.

"I know you're supposed to be here. But sometimes you have to exercise a little better judgment as a mother."

I held my tongue. No, I was being overly sensitive, I corrected myself. Ms. Sparks was just trying to be helpful. After all, she had raised four of her own.

"You may be right," I said over my shoulder as I took Jeff's hand to lead him to his classroom.

"You need not to be so hard on them—they're still babies," she called after me.

I nodded again in her direction and moved on down the hallway.

All during the service that followed, I turned the nursery worker's comments over in my mind. Did I bring them to church too often? Was I using poor judgment?

It had been a long Sunday and a long week. Both kids had had runny noses, from teething or colds, I couldn't decide. But Saturday they seemed symptom free. I was one of the youngest mothers in church. Did the rest of them think I couldn't take care of my babies?

Well, there was one thing I was sure I was doing right—I had tried to teach the kids to obey and be polite. Kids were never too young to begin to learn that. I'd heard all too often the criticisms of preacher's kids—how unruly they were, how spoiled, how privileged. That was one thing I intended to do right—teach my kids to behave. Maybe I brought them to church too often, but certainly no one could accuse me of not making them mind me or their teachers.

I tried to shake it off. But when we stood for the final prayer, I didn't have the foggiest idea what the sermon topic had been. I returned to the nursery to find both children playing fine. Relieved, I gathered up their shoes and bags and headed for the car. Their father had an after-church committee meeting, so we had time to kill while waiting for him.

Outside, a friend caught my attention and we struck up a conversation about the upcoming after-game party for the teenagers. With Lisa in my arms, bags hanging from both my shoulders, and one eye on my three-year-old as he chased another toddler round and round on the grass, my friend and I finalized our menu.

All of a sudden, I heard someone call my name, an adult someone.

I turned around to see an older, single lady coming toward me on the sidewalk. "Dianna, Dianna," her voice was excited. "Did you see what Jeff just did?"

I checked behind me to see where he was.

The woman whom I recognized as Betty, from fifth row,

center section, left end of the pew continued, "He just chunked a rock at my car."

"Oh, no. I'm so sorry." I automatically swung around to grab Jeff's arm as he ran past me once more, chasing his friend David. "I'm so sorry," I repeated to Betty. "I didn't see him. Did he hurt you? Or the car?"

"Well, no. It was just a pebble." I breathed easier, still hanging onto Jeff's arm as he swayed from side to side playing peek a boo with David around my skirt.

"Oh. Well, I'm sorry. I didn't see him pick up a rock."

"Well he *did*. I heard it. And it could have scratched my car! I heard it hit the door just as I was driving out of the parking lot."

Her eyes blazed. She stood with both hands on her hips, as if waiting for me to do something.

"Where did he find a rock?" I asked.

"Probably in that flower bed." She pointed to the pebbles lining the sidewalk.

"Mmm. Probably. I'm sorry," I offered another apology. "I'll talk to him about it when I get him to the car."

"Well, you should. That's dangerous."

"I understand. It's just that I've never had occasion to teach him not to throw a rock because he's never done it before."

"Well, you need to teach him. Kids need to be taught to behave."

"Yes, I, . . . I, ..." I could feel my eyes start to fill. "I'll talk to him and tell him it's dangerous to—"

"Well, I hope you spank him good." She turned on her heel, got back in her car, and drove away.

As we waited for the committee meeting to end, ours was the last family on the parking lot that evening. Lisa slept quietly in my arms. The sound of Jeff's snoring drifted from where he lay curled up in the backseat. But I stayed awake for the next forty-eight hours.

∾ ∾ ∾

He has a right to criticize who has a heart to help.
—*Abraham Lincoln*

When I am angry at myself, I criticize others.
—*Ed Howe*

The easiest faults to notice are the faults you don't have.
—*Unknown*

A smile in giving honest criticism can make the difference between resentment and reform.
—*Philip Steinmetz*

Words that Cast Doubt

*R*ealtor Ken Reimer recalls struggling with a math test in high school. That evening he came home to complain to his parents and a family friend about the difficulty of the test. The family friend, his mom's age, flopped down on the sofa beside him and looked him squarely in the face. "Ken, it only gets harder."

Ken took in the comment and turned it over in his mind. Could that be true?

In college, he decided that it was indeed true. His college tests proved to be much harder than those in high school. Home from college and complaining about his absent-minded professors and their surly demands, he again bumped into the family friend. She reminded him once again, "Ken, it only gets harder."

Could it be still harder than this?

In graduate school, he had other chances to verify the truth of her pronouncement and his predicament. Yes, he decided, his graduate exams were in fact only harder than those in his undergrad work.

Once he started his own business, Ken had other occasions to hit obstacles and run smack into those words again: "Ken, it only gets harder." With mortgages, kids, and clients, he continues to recall that ubiquitous refrain: "Ken, it only gets harder."

So is he discouraged today?

"No," he explains, "all I do is convert that comment in my head. When something's hard, I say to myself, 'If it only gets harder, this must be easy. I'll know that in retrospect.'"

So he digs in his heels and plows straight through the wall before him.

❧ ❧ ❧

Expect trouble as an inevitable part of life and repeat to yourself the most comforting words of all: This, too, shall pass.

—*Ann Landers*

The most immutable barrier in nature is between one man's thoughts and another's.

—*William James*

Words that Encourage

WHEN I GROW UP . . .

The promise was a long time keeping. But then, so was the dream.

In the early 1950s in a small Southern California town, a little girl hefted yet another load of books onto the tiny library's counter.

The girl was a reader. Her parents had books all over their home, but not always the ones she wanted. So she'd make her weekly trek to the yellow library with the brown trim, the little one-room building where the children's library actually was just a nook. Frequently, she ventured out of that nook in search of heftier fare.

As the white-haired librarian hand-stamped the due dates in the ten-year-old's choices, the little girl looked longingly at "The New Book" prominently displayed on the counter. She marveled again at the wonder of writing a book and having it honored like that, right there for the world to see.

That particular day, she confessed her goal.

"When I grow up," she said, "I'm going to be a writer. I'm going to write books."

The librarian looked up from her stamping and smiled, not with the condescension so many children receive, but with encouragement.

"When you do write that book," she replied, "bring it into our library and we'll put it on display, right here on the counter."

The little girl promised she would.

As she grew, so did her dream. She got her first job in ninth grade, writing brief personality profiles, which earned her $1.50 each from the local newspaper. The money palled in comparison with the magic of seeing her words on paper.

A book was a long way off.

She edited her high-school paper, married and started a family, but the itch to write burned deep. She got a part-time job covering school news at a weekly newspaper. It kept her brain busy as she balanced babies.

But no book.

She went to work full-time for a major daily. Even tried her hand at magazines.

Still no book.

Finally, she believed she had something to say and started a book. She sent it off to two publishers and was rejected. She put it away, sadly. Several years later, the old dream increased in persistence. She got an agent and wrote another book. She pulled the other out of hiding, and soon both were sold.

But the world of book publishing moves slower than that of daily newspapers, and she waited two long years. The day the box arrived on her doorstep with its free author's copies, she ripped it open. Then she cried. She'd waited so long to hold her dream in her hands.

Then she remembered that librarian's invitation and her promise.

Of course, that particular librarian had died years ago,

and the little library had been razed to make way for a larger incarnation.

The woman called and got the name of the head librarian. She wrote a letter, telling her how much her predecessor's words had meant to the girl. She'd been in town for her thirtieth high school reunion, she wrote, and could she please bring her two books by and give them to the library? It would mean so much to that ten-year-old girl, and seemed a way of honoring all the librarians who had ever encouraged a child.

The librarian called and said, "Come."

So she did, clutching a copy of each book.

She found the new looming library right across the street from her old high school, just opposite the room where she'd struggled through algebra, mourning the necessity of a subject that writers would surely never use, and nearly on top of that spot where her old house once stood, the neighborhood demolished for a civic center and this looming library.

Inside, the librarian welcomed her warmly. She introduced a reporter from the local newspaper—a descendant of the paper she'd begged a chance to write for long ago.

Then she presented her books to the librarian, who placed them on the counter with a sign of explanation. Tears rolled down the woman's checks.

Then she hugged the librarian and left, pausing for a picture outside, which proved that dreams can come true and promises can be kept. Even if it takes thirty-eight years.

The ten-year-old girl and the writer she'd become posed by the library sign, right next to the reader board, which said: "Welcome back, Jann Mitchell."

Jann Mitchell is a writer with the *Oregonian* in Portland, Oregon, and has four published books now: *Codependent for Sure, Organized Serenity, Home Sweeter*

Home: Creating a Haven of Simplicity and Spirit, and *Love Sweeter Love: Creating Relationships of Simplicity and Spirit.* The story above is one she herself wrote about the impact of that librarian's words on her dream.

✍ ✍ ✍

All words are pegs to hang ideas on.

—*Harriet Ward Beecher*

Encourage one another and build each other up.

—*1 Thessalonians 5:11*

Words that Divide

MIRROR, MIRROR, ON THE WALL . . .

*A*lthough the advertisers would have us believe we "never outgrow our need for milk," there is stronger sustenance for siblings. Children, whether eight or eighty, never outgrow their need to feel that their parents love them totally, unconditionally, uniquely.

I watched as my younger sister, Angie, played with her two young daughters near the Christmas tree. Always careful to treat them equitably and love them equally, Angie watched as the inevitable happened. The younger one got the most popular toy under the tree, a telephone set. It only took a few moments for a tug of war to develop between the three-year-old and the five-year-old, both wanting the phone.

There were cries of, "Mommy, talk to me on the phone."

Then, "No, Mommy, talk to *me* on the phone."

The older one yanked the phone once again out of her younger sister's lap and put it to her ear. She turned back to face her mom seated on the sofa. "Okay, Mom, I'm on the line. How are you today?"

The younger sister sat in the middle of the floor and continued to yelp, "It's *my* phone, Mommy. It's *my* phone."

All of a sudden her quick-thinking mom took the other receiver and responded to the older child. "Sarah, so glad you called. I'm fine today. Say, would you tell your little sister to quit crying and then put her on the line a moment?"

The older one turned to the younger. "Mom says to quit crying. And she wants to talk to you." Whereupon, the older daughter handed Sis the phone and stood patiently waiting for her own turn.

One of the biggest obstacles to feeling total acceptance from parents is when they show favoritism among their children. Ever since Rebekah plotted with beloved son Jacob and later when Joseph had his coat of many colors, parents have played havoc with their kids' psyches by showing favoritism to one child over another.

Even as an adult who runs her own manufacturing business, Maryanne has mixed feelings about the grandmother she loved deeply. On the surface, Maryanne's parents and grandparents made it a rule never to show favoritism to their children and grandchildren. They spent the same on their gifts. They raised them with the same rules. They attended all the same school celebrations and applauded equally loudly at the children's accomplishments. But at her grandmother's funeral, one longtime friend of her grandmother's commented to Maryanne after the memorial service, "I sure thought a lot of your grandmother, and I feel as though I know you. She talked of you constantly—all of her grandkids. But you know that you were her favorite, don't you?"

No, Maryanne hadn't known that before. And she didn't want to know it then. It spoiled the memories of childhood when all the siblings received their fair share of love and attention. That sense of impartiality had provided security.

It's a divisive thing—to know your parents have favorites—no matter whether you're the favored or the second-in-line.

Connie, age forty-two and married to a psychologist, shares her own memories of a household where she considered herself third-in-line. "Bradley was always my mother's favorite. He was the baby. She always felt that Dad was too hard on him because he was the boy. And when Dad would finish chewing Bradley out, Momma would hug him and tell him he was her favorite and bake him an apple pie. To this day, I feel sure that's why he has a weight problem.

"And Lydia was always Dad's favorite. When he'd go on business trips in the summer, he'd always take her with him. Never Bradley or me. Always Lydia. He thought she was the cutest thing when she'd sing. And he'd have her perform when we had company. Me—I was nobody's favorite, and I knew it. They didn't even argue that fact. It has taken me twenty-one years married to a psychologist to overcome those feelings of inferiority and self-doubt."

Even at age sixty-two the feeling doesn't disappear. Louise calls her only brother's widow almost weekly, crying and asking what more she can do for her emotionally distant, ninety-two-year-old mother. Mrs. Redmond, her mother, still in good health, lives alone on her farm where there's always something to be done—from mowing the pasture to trimming the trees to cleaning the garage. Louise makes the 500-mile trek every two weeks to help out, to take her mother grocery shopping, to shampoo and rebraid her hair, to restock her medications. When she's not there physically, she phones her mother every night—only to hear her complain that she's not doing enough.

Louise remembers standing at the casket of her older brother after his fatal heart attack, holding her mother's arm, comforting her in her grief. When friends and family circulated by the casket, Louise heard her mother say more than once to mourners, "Bill was a good man, a good son. Always was. He was always my favorite, you know."

Those words still bruise, batter, and embitter five years later.

❧ ❧ ❧

A great part of the mischiefs that vex this world arises from words.

—*Edmund Burke*

Live in peace with each other.

—*1 Thessalonians 5:13*

Words that Embarrass

MARS, NOT THE MOON

*H*ave you ever let your tongue roll before you put your mind in gear? Embarrassed yourself enough to wish for a big black hole to swallow you from sight? It happens.

I remember my year in Okinawa as a nineteen-year-old, working for the military education division. It took only a week or two to realize that my civilian boss, Joe J. Jellison, liked to tell a good story and play a practical joke. And when it came to business, as a lowly GS4 in the government classification system reporting to a GS16, I tried to absorb anything that came out of his mouth. From writing curriculum to helping soldiers pass their GED exams to pointing out where to buy Christmas gifts off post, he spoke with authority. I believed.

Standing in the doorway between our offices one day, he mentioned that his wife and sons would finally be traveling from Germany to join him on the island. We began talking about his past assignments. He then began to recall odd customs and tasteless foods around the globe while I took in every word. To say that I was uninitiated to travel and other cultures was a gross understatement at that point in my life, so I listened wide-eyed to his adventures. Then attention turned to our current locale, and he asked me where we'd found off-base housing.

"We're living at Kadena Circle," I answered. "And our quarters aren't much to write home about. This humidity, I'm just not used to it. The extra bedroom is so musty that mold is growing up the walls. I've got to find out what to do about it."

"The mold is the least of your worries," he said. "Have you seen the roaches over here?"

"No, I haven't." Yet another problem to tackle?

"They're huge."

My eyes grew bigger as this hulk of a leader leaned in the doorway and his disc jockey voice of authority continued.

"In fact, just the other night I heard something shuffling around. And sure enough, I crawled out of bed and walked into the living room. There was a roach pushing my shoe along on the floor."

"Really?" I asked.

At that Mr. Jellison doubled over in laughter.

Suffice it to say, it wasn't the last time he got me during my stint as his administrative assistant. And I wish I could say it was the last time such a gullible response ever left my lips and embarrassed me in front of someone.

But there was the time when I was a twenty-one-year-old sitting in a college English lecture. The professor recited a poem, whose title I've long forgotten, and droned on about the various poetic devices the author had used.

He paused on a metaphor and probed, "Why the word *eunuch* here? Can anyone tell me the meaning of *eunuch*?" He silently surveyed the class over the top of his bifocals, waiting.

His eyes stopped on me. Hadn't he told us that he graded on class participation? Say something, I thought.

I opened my mouth with the first thing that popped into mind: "Isn't that someone who guards kings, from Ethiopia? Like in the Bible—the Ethiopian eunuch."

Male students snickered across the room. When the professor regained his composure, he proceeded to define the word for us.

Embarrassing words seem to be the purview of both the young and the old.

My husband's seventy-two-year-old aunt recently confided to me about her ignorance of the facts of life during the 1940s when she was dating her later-to-be-husband. She had rushed into the house late one evening to tell her older sister about the date. Then she started to cry, "But I'm afraid I may be pregnant."

"You what?" Her sister demanded an accounting.

"He kissed me. What if I get pregnant? He kissed me before I could stop him."

She and her sister had a long talk.

From my own track record, you can understand why I try not to make others feel stupid when they say something equally absurd.

Several years ago when I was leading a training seminar for a utility company, we were waiting for all the participants to arrive on the first morning. I had placed the workshop materials and the course text, my first business book on technical writing, beside each tent-shaped name card on the tables. The early students sat thumbing through the binders and the book.

One man, who appeared to be about forty, flipped open my book and began to scan the jacket. "It says here on the

back of your book that you have several Fortune 500 clients."
I nodded. "I think my wife used to belong to that same
Fortune club."

Foolish, embarrassing comments happen not just to the
naïve, immature, meanspirited, or mentally challenged.

A congresswoman was touring the NASA facilities recently.
Because congressional representatives hold the purse strings
to space-exploration funding and are charged with the final
decisions about our national space program, the NASA
staffers were making an all-out effort to impress this particular
visitor and update her on the latest technology and issues.

During the trip, her tour guide rolled some actual footage
from the Pathfinder robot on the surface of Mars. As she
watched the video, the congressional dignitary seemed to be
trying to impress the reporters surrounding her with how
interested and informed she was. As the video footage ended,
the congresswoman commented to the NASA crowd following her. "That robot is so cool. Can you make it go over to
where they placed the flag?"

The staffer tried to swallow a guffaw. "This is *Mars*. . . .
That flag was on the moon."

❧ ❧ ❧

Communication is a measurable asset.
—*Susan Sampsell*

The difference between the right word and the
almost-right word is the difference between "lightning" and "lightning bug."
—*Mark Twain*

Words that Free

I'M HOME!

When Tom got an itch to move from Lincoln, Nebraska, to Sacramento, California, neither his wife nor his seventeen-year-old daughter shared his enthusiasm. So for weeks, he turned the decision over in his mind. Reason said it was the right thing to do. Rumor had it that his job at the local manufacturing plant would soon be history because of an impending merger. What's more, his friend who'd led the way to Sacramento months earlier called weekly to ask him to join his new start-up company.

What to do? Finally, ridding himself of the notion that his family would ever see the logic of the move and feeling the responsibility as sole supporter, he accepted the job. With reluctance, his wife packed. His daughter did not.

"I don't want to leave my friends!"

"I know you don't, but I've got to earn a living. And this job in Sacramento is my best chance to do that."

"But it's not fair. You're not being fair. It's my senior year!"

"Honey, I know. I understand. But I think it's important that we go as a family."

"No, it's not. It's not."

"I promise that we'll let you come back here to visit—often."

"How often?"

"Well, . . . often—as often as we can afford it."

Yvonne pressed him. "How often is that?"

"Every few weeks I hope."

She convulsed into tears and locked herself in her bedroom for days, coming out only to quit her part-time summer job at the movie theater.

A few weeks later, they loaded up their U-Haul and moved across country to the West Coast. Tom joined his friend in the new business, and things began to look up for them financially.

But neither his wife nor his daughter seemed to be adjusting. At nights, he lay in bed absorbing the cold silence. Why couldn't his wife understand? He'd tried to do the best he could for her. He lay awake and pondered a conversation that had transpired seventeen years earlier in the home of one of his high-school friends.

He and his friend Buddy had stopped by Buddy's house for Cokes after baseball practice one afternoon. His friend's mother walked into the kitchen, opened herself a Dr Pepper, and turned to glare at Tom. "Buddy says you and Alissa are going to get married next weekend."

"Yes. We are," he'd said. He felt stingy with the details, but what was to hide at this point? One passionate weekend, one big mistake, and the whole town knew.

"You kids are never going to make it. Couples who have to get married never do," she pronounced. And she walked out of the kitchen.

Tom had swallowed hard that afternoon and kept his mouth shut. But those words had echoed through the years time and time again when they'd come to difficult points in their marriage. But they'd proved Buddy's mother wrong—they *had* made it. Twenty-six years. For twenty-six years he'd been trying to do the right thing. And he had grown to love Alissa and Yvonne more than life itself.

As if reading his mind, his wife reached over in the darkness and squeezed his hand. He took it to mean that she was through with her long pout. And none too soon. He kissed her and eventually he fell asleep.

Yvonne remained the bigger problem. Once a month for eight straight months, he drove her to the airport and put her on a plane for Nebraska to spend the weekend with her friends there. And each weekend she returned home crying and angry, with some version of the same message: "You're ruining my life."

Tom was beginning to believe it. Late one January Sunday, he sat alone at the airport waiting for his daughter's returning plane. It had been a long, difficult week at work, and he faced a tougher week come Monday morning. In his job trying to sign on corporate clients for his friend's limo service, he charted new territory every day. Selling had never been his strong suit. It still proved tough to bring in new customers when the fledgling company had few references and a small fleet of cars. Why had he ever thought he could make it out here?

As he watched the passengers appear at the ramp doorway and move toward their loved ones, he waited, head hung low. Had he ruined his daughter's life as she continued to tell him? Would she hate him forever? And what about her future—college? She was threatening not to go at all. How sincere was the threat? Was she making the threat simply because she knew he had been saving for her education all her life? And what if she decided to go but wanted to move back to Nebraska to go to the University? He could never afford to be able to see her often enough—to fly her back and forth and pay tuition and room and board all the while.

And another thing, the checkbook. He felt it protruding from his jacket pocket. How much longer could they afford these monthly flights? Why had he promised her? He couldn't remember breaking his word to her, but neither had a previous promise been so expensive. Maybe it had been wrong for them to come to Sacramento after all. Maybe, as Yvonne had shouted at him on occasion, it was selfishness on his part. God only knew that he didn't think that was his motivation. But this daughter, who was a bright young woman, tortured him with her unhappiness.

Just then Yvonne appeared at the gate and walked toward him. He stood and greeted her with, "How was your flight?" Then he reached for her luggage.

Instead of the usual silence, she fell into his arms, sobbing. He wrapped his arms around her and thought his heart would break. Why was he doing this to her?

"Honey," he whispered to her. "I'm hating this. I'm so sorry. Maybe we should just—"

"No, dad." She pulled away from him and looked up into his eyes. "That's not why I'm crying. What I'm crying about is, I'm happy that I'm home." She nodded her head as if to reassure him that he'd heard correctly. "I'm really, finally home this time—here with you and mom."

The chains around his heart fell off. Four years later she graduated from college and met and married her husband in Sacramento.

❧ ❧ ❧

We were kids when everything was the kids' fault. Now we're parents when everything is the parents' fault.

—*Farm Journal*

Words that Discern

WILL WORK FOR FOOD

I zipped my car into the Albertson's parking lot and headed into the supermarket for the week's groceries. Just as I came out of the store, piled my groceries into the backseat of the car, and started the engine, I was startled by a knock against my window. I glanced around to see a man staring at me through the pane. He was thirtyish, rather shabbily dressed, with a few days' black stubble.

I hesitated a moment, not sure whether it was safe to roll down the window. Glancing around the parking lot, I noticed a few passersby in other aisles. After all, it was broad daylight and help was only a scream away. I lowered the window.

"Yes?" I asked as he peered in at me.

"I'm sorry to trouble you, ma'am. But I'm a little down on my luck, and I was wondering if you could spare some money or if you had a job for me."

"Hmmm." My automatic response when I need time to think things over. He seemed sober, coherent, and able-bodied.

He continued, "We really need food for the baby. That's

my wife and baby over there in that car. I lost my job, and we're having a hard time getting by just now."

I glanced in the rearview mirror to where he pointed. Through the windshield I spotted an older model car. Inside, sure enough, was a woman holding a tiny baby in her arms in the front seat. She nodded in my direction as if to add her plea to his.

My first response was to hand him a few crisp bills. After all, giving money to a special drive, donating used clothing or furniture to a mission, buying turkeys at Thanksgiving or children's toys for an angel tree at Christmas always gave me a warm, fuzzy feeling.

But something else popped into my mind. Was this a legitimate claim? How could I know? If so, he needed more than a handout; he needed a job. I began to roll names of other small business owners through my mind. Who would have a job? What kind of work was he looking for?

"Yes, I think I can help you," I said to him through the open window. "You said you were looking for work? I live less than two miles from here. Why don't you and your wife follow me to my house. I have some work there. The yard needs mowing. My husband has been traveling, and there are a few other odds and ends we need help with in the garage. I could pay you $100 to mow the lawn and—"

He dropped his hand from my car door and backed away. I ducked my head slightly to get a better look. Where was he? He'd suddenly disappeared from sight. I glanced back through my rearview mirror to see him dashing across the lot. Was he going to follow me? But why hadn't he said something? That was strange, just backing away without any response at all.

I pulled out of the parking slot and paused to look toward the car he'd singled out as his. The car was parked at the far side of the lot, away from the others. But he wasn't getting into the car. He said something to the woman through the window and continued to stand outside. I pulled up a few feet and waited longer. He just stood there, never moving to get inside the car. Then as I edged closer to the exit driveway to pull onto the freeway, I watched him approach another customer in the parking lot as he headed toward his car. And then another. And then another.

How often do you see people standing on the street, begging for money? Selling flowers? Offering to work for money to buy their baby milk? Each time I pass by, I reevaluate my attitude. Doesn't the Bible have a lot to say about helping the poor? "If you have done it unto the least of these, you have done it unto me?"

In addition to the ones and twos on the street corner—situation unknown—it seems that every team or every organization has its own cause. In the past two months, I've received letters, calls, or e-mails from friends and colleagues asking for my participation in the heart disease fund campaign, a breast cancer foundation benefit, the spinal-cord injury research fund, and the AIDS walkathon. Additionally, our local radio stations ask us to pledge to keep them on the air, and our politicians ask for our personal and financial support to help them clean up America and return integrity to government. All are worthy causes that desperately need our support.

But personal decisions come into play when others start to judge our responses, intentions, values, and motives. For example, some time ago, in the Letters to the Editor section of a national magazine, I read someone's tirade against the doctors of America. It seems that the letter writer had requested that a doctor in her community perform eye surgery on a needy child and the doctor had refused. The letter writer had been infuriated and lambasted doctors everywhere for being a greedy, hardhearted lot, who couldn't spare two hours to save the eyesight of a child.

The plea and righteous indignation seemed justified— until someone responded on behalf of the doctor, writing about the many hours of free medical care that the doctor devoted to the underprivileged in various community projects. I also know a doctor who has his own private plane and recruits his colleagues, specialists in their respective areas of medicine, to fly with him monthly to various countries in South America to offer free medical attention in the poorest villages.

Help the poor; discourage the swindlers. More than ever, requests from and for those in need have become a major area for discerning words and wise responses.

✎ ✎ ✎

The wise in heart are called discerning.
—*Proverbs 16:21*

Words that Hover

NAME THAT TUNE

Lynne Ritchie never considered herself an outcast, but then she never pictured herself in Carnegie Hall either.

Three weeks into seventh grade, her choir teacher asked her to stay after class. When the others left the room, the teacher minced few words: "You can't sing in choir."

Lynne's face fell. "Why?"

"I'm going to move you to study hall this period."

"But why?" A straight-A student, surely she hadn't been mistaken for somebody who needed extra tutoring during study hall.

Mrs. Waymire finished writing out the pink transfer slip and waved it toward her.

"But why?" Lynne persisted.

"Because you have the kind of voice that's going to get the others off-key."

Well, so much for sugarcoated words. That was news to Lynne, who'd enjoyed singing up until that exact moment. The choir was 130 students strong, and she was going to get them all off-key? She looked incredulously at her teacher. The teacher's grim expression never wavered.

Lynne turned and walked out of the choir room. She had just been assigned to never-never land. On the following day, she joined five other students in the study hall. One other girl who had been banished, Lynne presumed, because she'd joined the school late in the year, glanced in her direction and then returned to her book. The other four were boys Lynne recognized as hoodlums who spent most of their days in the principal's office and their nights on the street.

What was she to do? Lynne joined the group of fifth-period vagabonds.

Forty years later, Lynne recalls that they "bonded" for the year during this daily hour as choir outcasts. At the end of the year, she remained a good student, the other girl dropped out of school altogether, and the four "hoodlums" continued to create havoc around town.

To this day, Lynne still feels too self-conscious to sing aloud. Even in the shower.

❧ ❧ ❧

It is ridiculous for any man to criticize the works of another if he has not distinguished himself by his own performance.

—*Joseph Addison*

Wise men talk because they have something to say; fools because they have to say something.

—*Plato*

Words that Defend

NOT THE KATLIN I KNOW

*Y*ou remember Katlin, don't you?" Meredith prodded over lunch with an ex-coworker. Donna had worked with both Meredith and Katlin for six years but had left the organization when her husband took a job in another state. Upon her return during a holiday visit to the family, she had dialed the old office phone number and Meredith had answered. As the only one of the original troupe still working in the department, Meredith was glad to hear from Donna. They decided to have lunch together and catch up on old times.

"Katlin? Of course, I remember her. She was a doll. What's new in her life?"

Meredith elaborated: "Well, she's moved on. She's selling real estate now because she wanted to have more control of her time and schedule."

"Don't we all?"

"I think the biggest motivator, however, was the problem with her children."

"Oh? They were such neat kids whenever I was around them."

"Things have changed. The older son is a senior at State now, but he's really been giving them problems. Something about credit card debt. He ducked out on some loans they'd cosigned for, and they were left holding the financial bag. Then their middle child—the daughter, Dena—has run away from home several times. At one point last year, she took off across the country for almost a month with a boyfriend, and they didn't even know where she was for a long time."

"Oh, how sad."

Meredith continued the saga: "Then the younger one, Jamie—that's the one that used to come by the office so often after school—he somehow got off track with the wrong crowd. At one time Katlin thought he might be dabbling in drugs. I know drinking was a problem too."

"Oh, that's terrible. I'm so sorry. She must be heartbroken."

"She is. My heart goes out to her. It's just such a puzzle," Meredith agreed, but the tone of her voice didn't match the words. She added, "Kids really need a parent's undivided attention these days."

Donna was quiet for a long moment, as if not quite sure how to react to the news update or what was meant by all the details. Did Meredith have a hidden message there somewhere?

Then suddenly she leaned forward and slammed the lid on her surmise: "Well, . . . I guess it just goes to prove that even the very best parents can have kids turn out wrong."

☙ ☙ ☙

Tact is the art of making a point without making an enemy.

—*Howard W. Newton*

Whatever is in the heart overflows into speech.

—*Luke 6:45 lb*

Words that Haunt

WHERE THE RESEMBLANCE ENDS

At a recent family reunion, the adults gathered in the backyard at the old home place and swapped stories of their growing-up years. As the conversation began, an eaves-dropper would have thought they were a group of stand-up comics.

"Do you remember the time somebody wrapped our house in toilet paper and it rained?" someone recalled and then recounted the scene.

And then another: "Do you remember that time we all piled into that old army jeep and drove to Devil's Island for the weekend, and Kathy swallowed that turtle?"

Followed by another: "What about when Uncle Aaron found us out behind his shop with his power tools burned out and his scrap lumber all nailed together?"

One by one, the tales tumbled out. But as the sun fell lower in the sky, their reminiscences turned more somber. Finally, the brothers and sisters, cousins and kids, aunts and uncles turned to soul work and squabbles long swept under the rug for the sake of family harmony.

As if a blanket had snuggly wrapped them in the warm glow of family unity, they continued to confess grudges and hurts and offer forgiveness and healing.

In turn, Mike, the baby of the five children, finally spoke up. "Well, there's something . . . I guess I want to say too."

He had earned the reputation as the "quiet one." The others waited for him to continue.

"I always hated it when you all told me I was just like my father."

There was a pregnant silence. That was the one still-taboo topic in the family. Their father had been an abusive alcoholic who'd finally shot their mother and then himself when Mike was still in high school.

An aunt broke the uneasy silence. "Mike, when did anybody ever say that to you?"

"When?" Mike looked astonished that she didn't remember. "All the time. Everybody. All of you. For years. All the time I was growing up. From the time I was a little bitty kid, everybody would pat me on the head or on the rump, and say, 'You're just like your father.' I hated to hear that. I never wanted to be like him. I still don't."

The aunt started to shake her head. "Oh, no. I never meant that . . . I mean, yes, I've said it a thousand times, but I never meant what you thought. I meant that you *looked* like your father—his blue eyes, his freckles, his blond hair, his dimples. But I never meant that you *acted* like him."

Mike surveyed the faces of the family members gathered around him in the backyard. One by one, they echoed the same meaning. "Yeah, your chin," said one. "And your ears," said another. Their eyes confirmed the truth of what the aunt said.

"Oh," this man of fifty said as he settled back into silence—with a much less intense set of his jaw.

❧ ❧ ❧

The tongue that brings healing is a tree of life.
—*Proverbs 15:4*

Words that Needle

TENNIS NOT-TOS

*E*very time executive Zane Canon takes to the tennis court, he wraps his hand around the racket just so. Then he swings against the air, readjusts, swings, readjusts, swings, readjusts. Five, fifteen, fifty times. It's never enough to feel as though he's mastered his serve. Why?

Zane routinely volleyed on the tennis court after school most afternoons with his friend Tim. Both had dreams of being the next tennis superstar on the circuit. But Tim, Zane decided, definitely had a better shot at those dreams because his mom also taught history at their junior high. And she occasionally took to the tennis court after the school day to mentor her son.

Tim and Zane were on the courts one particular Tuesday afternoon. When Zane straightened up from chasing a runaway ball, he saw Tim's mom walk up to the court next to theirs. Without a greeting, she motioned for Tim to join her.

"Zane, see you later. My mom's here. She's gonna help me with my serve."

"Yeah, see ya," Zane said, as he began to bounce the ball against the nearby backboard. So why couldn't she help him too?

Oh, well. Zane continued to slam the tennis ball against the backboard and then maneuver from side to side to return it. Then it occurred to him that he could hear, watch, and learn just by being a shadow.

He edged closer and closer until their faint conversation became clearly audible. Then he leisurely began to serve his ball against the backboard to feign disinterest in the mentoring session on the nearby court.

It didn't work. With each thud against the board, he missed a key word. He stopped for a moment to glance around for other possibilities.

Okay, so what was wrong with just standing on the court next to Tim and his mom? He could listen and try to imitate what she was telling him. He walked over closer to the duo.

He had not been there but a moment when he heard Tim's mother say to him, "Stop a minute. Just stand here and watch Zane serve."

Well, how about that, Zane thought. She's telling *him* to watch *me*. He raised his racket high over his right shoulder and served the ball hard into the opposite court, purely for their benefit.

Then he heard Tim's mother say, "Did you see that? Well, don't *ever* hold your racket like he does."

She then turned her back to him and walked away with her son to a new court.

The senior executive still wonders, "So why didn't she tell me the *right* way?" When he plays a match with a client, he can still hear her admonition: "Don't *ever* hold your racket like he does."

Sometimes it helps to bare troubles rather than bear them.

—*Lloyd Cory*

Words that Teach

YELL POLITELY

*D*arla approached the day-care center with her two toddlers in tow and her five-week-old in her arms. Her part-time, three days a week job was now going to be an exercise in time management and patience. Fortunately, her husband's schedule allowed him to be home most of the time with the children during the hours she worked. But on the few occasions when he couldn't, her next best option was taking them to day care.

As they approached the door, the four-year-old reached out to open it for his mom and brothers. But from behind them, a man's extended arm reached it before the four-year-old's did.

"I'll get that," the man's voice from behind them said as he held the door open.

"No! No!" Alex screamed. "I wanted to get it! I wanted to get it!" The four-year-old threw himself on the floor and began to kick his feet. "I wanted to open the door. It's *my* mommy."

Embarrassed, Darla thanked the stranger holding the door for their entourage and tried with one free hand to retrieve her four-year-old from the floor. She had never seen him pitch such a fit.

"Alex, what's the matter with you? Stand up. Why are you acting like that?"

"No, no, I wanted to open the door. *I* open the doors for you."

"Yes, Alex, you do. But that man opened it for us this time. You're supposed to say thank you."

"No, no, *I* wanted to open the door." He continued to wail as she dragged him down the hallway toward the check-in center. "I want to be polite. I want to open the door!"

Darla could only hope no one she knew was looking. She continued to try to drag him along with one arm, with the two-year-old tagging along and the baby crying in her arms. "Alex, stand up. Stand up and walk."

"I want to be polite," Alex continued to scream. "You told me I could be polite and open the door for you."

"Alex, yes, you can be polite. But that man did us a favor. He held the door for us because he was polite too."

"No, no, *I* want to be polite." Alex continued to drag his feet, screaming and kicking down the hallway. Darla could not remember his ever having acted this way. She had delivered the two-year-old to his room, and Alex was still tugging, pushing, and whining. This had gone on way too long.

She turned and headed back out to the car without leaving either Alex or the baby at the day-care center. A *60 Minutes* TV special the night before on how violence affected children had gotten her attention. Was this just the beginning of Alex's acting out the violence he had seen in cartoons? She strapped the baby and Alex into the backseat and drove straight home.

Once there, she began to explain to Alex that she intended to rid his closet of all his toys that were associated with violence. Wide-eyed, Alex sat on the sofa and watched her clean out his toy chest.

Then she sat down with him for a long talk about the incident at the day-care center.

He started the whimpering again, "But you told me *I* could be polite and open the doors for you. I don't want him to open the door. *I* want to be polite."

"Yes, Alex, I did tell you that you could open the door. And that's what polite boys do. But that man was just helping us out. He was being polite to all of us. The next time somebody opens a door for us, here's what you're supposed to say . . . You say, 'Thank you. I'll get the next one.' And then you can open the next door we come to."

"Oh," Alex said. The tears and whimpering suddenly stopped. "Oh."

It's the daily sessions that build life's lessons.

❦ ❦ ❦

Train a child in the way he should go, and when he is old he will not turn from it.

—*Proverbs 22:6*

Words that Nudge

QUIPS AND QUOTES, NOT "QUIT"

*B*efore the old home burned to the ground, Wanda Richerson grabbed one item that remains to this day stuck in the corner of the framed photo of her mother, who passed away in 1995 at the age of seventy-six.

Wanda grew up in the sixties in a haven of calm. Her parents, Melvin and Doris Kunkel, were married fifty-two happy years, during which Wanda never heard an argument between them. And although her mother liked an immaculate house, she had a rather unique way of keeping it that way.

She refused to nag. Nudge, yes. Nag, never. She never griped at her husband or daughter over the petty little things that often alienate family and friends.

Instead, she captured her wishes and dreams in words of wisdom and wit—said by somebody else. Copying well-known quotations and quips, she posted them prominently on the bathroom mirror, the central station at some hour of the day for every member of the family. Had Post-it notes been invented back then, Doris Kunkel most certainly would have bought stock in 3M.

The yellowed note, in her mother's handwriting and still covered with Scotch tape, remains posted in the corner of the photo at the end of the hall in Wanda's home: "Don't put it down; put it away."

It's a slogan Wanda still uses to "nudge" her girls, her husband, and their household.

❧ ❧ ❧

The most valuable of all talents is never using two words when one will do.

—*Thomas Jefferson*

Words that Rattle

IF YOU'RE SO SMART, WHY AIN'T YOU RICH?

*H*ave you ever taken downers? No, not drugs. I'm referring to the kind of comments that bring your spirit down. You get a promotion. You make the big sale. You decide to start your own business. You go back to school for that degree. You pull up stakes and move across country.

Then someone you know says to you, "That's crazy." Or, "I hope you know what you're doing." Or, "I hope you're not disappointed," in a tone that sounds as though you soon will be.

Then these people go on to share examples of failures they've known. They question your judgment. They doubt you'll achieve the outcome you planned. They tell you that you'll need more money than you estimate. They point out the downside, the disadvantages, and the disappointments that are about to crop up along the way.

What you'd like to hear on such occasions is something akin to these comments: "What spunk! Way to go!" Or, "What can I do to help you with that?" Or, "I wish I had the courage you have!" Or, "I'll be praying that it works out just as you want it to."

Parents and friends can sometimes be the worst when it comes to downers. It's not that they're trying to hold you back; it's often that they fear for your future. If the status quo is livable and predictable, why, they think, should you cause worry by changing things?

Other people have a more sinister mind-set: They have low self-esteem and lack courage themselves. They have a low opinion of your talents and judgment. Or they envy your ability, foresight, or circumstances.

But the downers do cause doubt, even for the strongest decision makers among us.

That's when you have to apply the old if-you're-so-smart-why-ain't-you-rich rule. That is, look carefully at the messengers: What is their lifestyle? How successful are they at what they do? What is their general attitude about others more success-ful or fortunate than they are? How genuinely happy do they appear to be? Do they walk close to the Lord and often—or seldom—speak His mind?

Answers to those questions give you big clues about the motivation behind their morose messages to you.

If you find yourself slapped by a downer, rise above the remarks and go to work on the proof of the speaker's error in judgment. You may find these words helpful: "You could be right about what I'm about to do. I'll try to remember that you warned me. And I'll keep you posted on what's happen-ing along the way. If things turn out much better than you expect, do you want me to let you know that also?"

☙ ☙ ☙

Children should be careful what they say—parents are always repeating what they hear.

—*Unknown*

He can compress the most words into the smallest idea of any man I ever met.

—*Abraham Lincoln*

The wise in heart are called discerning, and pleasant words promote instruction. A wise man's heart guides his mouth, and his lips promote instruction.

—*Proverbs 16:21, 23*

Words that Thank

NO FINGERS BUT A GRATEFUL HEART

When she took her young daughter Lilly back to Orthopedic Hospital for her eighth amputation, Dottie Walters was at the lowest ebb of her life. She couldn't stop crying. Outwardly or inwardly.

Her young daughter's hand had been crushed in a terrible accident while she was riding on the back of a forklift her father had rented to move hay for their horses. The steering gear broke as she was going down a hill, and the rig turned over, pinning Lilly beneath, with the weight of the rig on her left hand. Gangrene set in.

As they walked down the long bleak corridor toward the new hospital room, all that ran through Dottie's mind was the *can'ts*. She'll never play a musical instrument. She'll never type. She'll never toss her own little baby girl into the air and gurgle with her. She'll never . . . and the list went on.

"Hi, I'm Toni Daniels," the teenager in the next bed greeted them when they walked into their double-occupancy room— "home" for the next few days. "I've been waiting for you! I need you to go back down the hall before you unpack. There's a little boy down there who just came in. Bad accident. You need to go down there and cheer him up. Third room on the left."

Neither Dottie nor Lilly expected that to be their first order upon admission. Nevertheless, this teenager had a personality that filled the room. What else was there to do but wait for a hospital gown and someone to draw blood?

They unloaded their things into the tiny closet and did as the teenager had asked.

When they returned, Toni bubbled on. She told them about attending a high school for handicapped students. "You're never handicapped as long as you can help someone else. I've got a friend at my school, born with no legs or arms, and he teaches the typing class!"

Toni's words slapped Dottie to attention. Within minutes, she was down the hall at the pay phones, calling IBM. "I've got to have that book—the one-hand typing book." The manager on the other end of the line arranged for Lilly to receive the one-hand touch-typing book that Toni had told them about.

Days later after Lilly's surgery, they said their goodbyes to Toni and checked out of the hospital, without understanding the impact her information would have on them through the years.

That typing book forever altered Dottie's attitude, as well as her daughter's life. In the ensuing years, Lilly has become an accomplished actress and singer, so graceful, confident, and strong that most people never even notice the missing fingers.

But how to say thanks to someone who has given you a new future?

Dottie and Lilly puzzled over the predicament of the "missing" angel in their lives. For years, they have run a successful speaker's bureau in Glendora, California, but they never were able to locate Toni again to offer their thanks. You may have read this much of Lilly and Dottie's story in *Second Helping of Chicken Soup for the Soul,* the bestseller from Jack Canfield and Mark Victor Hansen.

But Toni Daniels had not.

My friends Dottie and Lilly Walters had tried many times since that initial hospital meeting to get in touch with Toni. But they found no trace of the person they'd come to refer to as their angel. And no way to say thanks. Until the idea of writing their story in the *Chicken Soup* book. When *Second Helping of Chicken Soup for the Soul* hit the bookstores, thousands of letters from parents and rehab people all over the United States and Canada arrived, thanking them for the hope shared through their story. Many wanted to order the one-hand typing book, with which Lilly encloses her personal letter of encouragement to the recipient. The typing book continued to be their way of passing on their thanks through encouraging others.

But still no trace of Toni, their angel.

Then in the fall of 1998, Dottie received a call at her bureau office. When she answered, the voice on the other end of the line said, "My students keep telling me that I'm featured in a book. I didn't believe them, but finally I went to a bookstore and bought the book."

Dottie gasped.

"They were right," the voice continued. "I'm the one. I'm Toni Daniels."

Finally, Dottie and Lilly had their opportunity to thank her in person and tell her Paul Harvey's "the rest of the story." Toni took a few days off from her position as Director of Admissions and Recruitment with the General Theological Seminary of the Episcopal Church in New York City and flew out to Glendora for a visit. Then their "angel" received thanks from grateful hearts once again by being featured in the Walters' magazine, *Sharing Ideas.*

I often wonder about the biblical account of the ten lepers who were healed. Only one returned to say thank you. The Master asked, "Were not all ten cleansed? Where are the other nine?"

☙ ☙ ☙

He who forgets the language of gratitude can never be on speaking terms with happiness.

—*C. Neil Strait*

Words that Tease

PAYDAY

The foursome finished the game and began to stack the dominoes back in the box. The two wives had teamed up against the two husbands and had beat them royally—not an unusual occurrence during the last twenty years. They continued to banter back and forth about the risks taken and lost during the earlier games.

Then conversation turned to Christmas: the shopping left to do, the food to prepare for company, the cards yet to be signed.

"And that reminds me," one wife said to her friend. "I bet Wayne hasn't bought my gift yet." Then to him, "Have you?"

Husband Wayne shook his head, took her hand in his hand, and in playful fashion kissed it like a Frenchman. "What more could you ask than living with me? You want a gift too?"

The second wife said, "Well, Burt's out of the doghouse. He remembered our anniversary last week." She stuck out her hand to show off her new garnet ring to their friends.

"I noticed that earlier, but I wasn't sure it was new," her friend said, oohing and aahing over it.

Then with a glance back toward her own husband, who still held her hand, she continued to her friend, "Wayne never gets me anything—except at Christmas. He never buys me a birthday present. He never buys me an anniversary present. He never buys me a Valentine's gift. Only Christmas." She took both his hands in hers and squeezed before letting go. "But he does all right by me for Christmas."

The other couple glanced Wayne's way to see if that were an exaggeration. To their questioning expressions, Wayne simply shrugged his shoulders sheepishly.

Wayne's wife continued, "But I have it figured out. Yeah, after forty years together, I've figured it out. So it doesn't bother me anymore. He grew up on a farm—they got all their income at the *end* of the year. He forgets he has money in the bank *all* year long. That's why he only remembers to spend it at Christmas."

Her husband looked at her a moment, his eyes twinkling. "You're right," he agreed. "Sounds logical."

Then he leaned across the game table toward her, his face inches from hers: "And I understand that *you* get paid . . . every *two weeks*—should I expect a package Friday?"

Warm words make cozy beds.

◆ ◆ ◆

I never used words like "sexy" in the 20's. To me, that was like talking about toilets. I preferred to use words like "romantic" when a man sent flowers or poems.

—*Gloria Swanson*

Words that Warm

FOUR HUSBANDS AND A VEIL

Vicky Ulrich surveyed the sea of suntanned male faces in her Yemen classroom. It was not a culture in which American women felt quickly comfortable. She and her husband, employed by an American oil company, had studied the customs of the culture before arriving. And although she was quite familiar with the Arab views of how women should dress, behave, and speak in public, familiarity did not breed acceptance. She understood that all too well.

The men and women before her had come to her classes from all walks of life—engineers, professors, accountants—to perfect their English at the Yemen-American Language Institute. She drew in her breath and tried to relax. This was the platform to test her mettle.

Suddenly a sober-faced male engineer spoke to her gruffly in front of the group. "Are you aware that many of us have four wives?"

Understanding this first question as a test to her acceptance of them personally and of her ability to hold her own in a group of men, she thought a moment and then brightened:

"What a country! I think I'll go out and find a few more husbands!"

By the end of that first class, they had become her students in the real sense of the word. But to be accepted, however, was not all Vicky hoped to accomplish while there.

Night after night, woman after woman approached her informally about their difficulty with the customs of their country and the restrictions society placed on them. Only the brightest and the richest found their way into her classroom. Day after day, she empathized with the voices behind the veils.

But it was hard to think of them as individuals when she could not see their faces. With faces veiled, hair covered, hands gloved, and black *abayas* flowing past the ankles, she could recognize who was talking to her only by glancing down at the speaker's shoes. Shoes and voices became the women's classroom ID.

She longed to help even these few to shed customs that they felt unreasonable, antiquated, and even unhealthy. Their bodies remained pale and frail, lacking vitamin D from the sunshine. Their veils and gloves became unsanitary.

When they complained about this "protection" that their fathers or husbands ordered them to wear, Vicky tried to respond with suggestions and encouragement.

"Please, if there's any way you can persuade your fathers or husbands or brothers, ask them to permit you to come to class without your veils. I can't help you with your English pronunciation as well as I could if I could see your lips when you speak. I need to see your tongue, mouth, and lips move."

Secretly, she envisioned throngs of brothers, husbands, and fathers descending on her classroom to put a stop to her "inflammatory" remarks and Western values. But she never let on to the women that she feared recrimination.

Instead, they shared their common frustration through laughter and jokes together in the classroom. It was a fine line

Vicky felt she was walking—acceptance of their culture and yet empathy with their individual situations and dreams.

During their semester together, some women became successful in persuading the men in their lives to let them uncover their faces; others did not.

One day at the shopping center toward the end of her tenure in the country, Vicky was strolling along looking for fresh fruits and vegetables when she heard a voice behind her, trying to get her attention. She turned around but saw no one she knew.

Instead, a young woman stood face-to-face with her, eyes twinkling, waiting patiently.

Vicky stared puzzled. Should she know this woman? Obviously, she wasn't an old acquaintance from the States; she was Yemeni. But Vicky could not place her face among her school administrators or staff, the church group, her husband's employees, or her neighborhood.

"Teacher Vicky, what's the matter?" the woman giggled. "Don't you recognize me?"

Vicky glanced down at her shoes. "Semira?"

They fell into each other's arms, laughing as they remembered the dreams shared through the warmth of their classroom discussions.

❧ ❧ ❧

Blessed are the peacemakers.

—*Matthew 5:9*

The more you say, the less people remember.

—*Anatole France*

It's often better to slip with your foot than with your tongue.

—*Boys' Life*

Words that Trap

HOLD THE CHEESE

Sometimes we believe that others control our lives, that others look down on us, that others don't like us, that others "have it in for us." On first blush, those ideas protect us from having to face unpleasant things about ourselves that we need to change.

Then again, maybe those words don't protect us—maybe they trap us. Sometimes for a lifetime.

Art dealer Mark Nettles recalls a conversation he had with a staff sergeant during his stint in language school during his army days. Sergeant Patty Filbein seldom gave her new recruits their P.T. (physical training) tests. According to her, it wasn't that she didn't like to rise and shine at 5:00 A.M.; it was that she couldn't "give them enough workout to do them any good."

About noon one day, Mark jogged in from a seven-mile run and uncapped a bottle of water to replenish what was oozing out of every pore in his body. He stood in front of the counter, waiting on his sergeant to finish her phone call before he asked to see the day's duty roster.

Perched atop a stool behind the check-in counter with her back toward Mark, Sergeant Filbein continued her phone conversation. "They're crazy. So why do they think I can pass a P.T. test? I'm big boned." She held up a wrist as if to reassess that conclusion again for herself. "Yeah. . . . Right. . . . Uh-huh."

Mark cleared his throat, but she didn't seem to hear him standing behind her.

She continued, "The army weight and P.T. standards are as ridiculous as everything else around here." She shifted the phone to the other ear. "Right." Her head kept bobbing. "No way. . . . Well, they're not going to kick me out for some stupid standard that's impossible to meet. I'm big boned and those exercises are impossible to do if you're my size. What do they expect?"

Just then another staffer came hustling through the lobby. He called to her, "Sergeant Filbein, I'm going for lunch. You want me to bring you something?"

She covered the telephone receiver and yelled back, "Yeah. Bring me a large pizza, everything on it. And extra cheese. And a strawberry malt!"

When she turned around to yell the last order, Mark caught her attention.

"Gotta go," she said into the phone and slammed it back on the cradle. "Didn't see you standing there, Nettles."

He chug-a-lugged the rest of his bottle of water and then remarked, "It's hot out there this morning."

"You're lucky."

"Lucky?"

"Because you like to exercise."

"I don't *like* to exercise, Sergeant Filbein. . . . Nobody *likes* to exercise. I just like the results."

She stared at him blankly.

Three years later, Sergeant Filbein's ten-year army career ended. She was released from duty for not maintaining weight and physical training standards.

⚭ ⚭ ⚭

Most of us really want to be half-understood. Not to be understood at all is frustrating; to be wholly understood is humiliating.

—*Sydney Harris*

I think we have too many high-sounding words and too few actions that correspond with them.

—*Abigail Adams*

Words that Heal

FOR THE SAKE OF SISTERS

*I*n their childhood, they were inseparable companions. In their later years, they are soul mates. Something happened in the middle.

As sisters growing up, Bonnie and Bubbles presented a united front to the world of reality: the 1929 stock market crash, a decade of depression, and the Second World War. It was Bubbles that first suggested they roll their socks down around their ankles once they walked to the bottom of the hill and around the curve. After all, what Daddy couldn't see wouldn't hurt him. And rolled-down socks made life so much easier for them at school.

They were satisfied to get only apples, oranges, and nuts at Grandpa's on Christmas morning. After all, they had each other for so many more important adventures than such simple treats afforded.

Although three years apart in age, as teens they often double-dated. And when Bonnie and Wilbur married, Bubbles and Franklin "stood up" for them. They became a foursome for their twenties. And as three kids came along to each couple, the sisters served as surrogate mothers to each other's brood at least weekly.

But farm life grew harder and harder for both families. The prosperity of the '50s that provided some families with white picket fences and debutante balls for their daughters eluded them. Bonnie went to work as a secretary in a manufacturing plant; Bubbles got a job on the assembly line at the same plant.

Family finances grew thinner as the children's needs expanded. It seemed like every time they got together, Bonnie and Bubbles soon found themselves in an argument. It was family sickness, stress, the times.

"You think you're better than I am, don't you?" Bubbles said to her sister one day as they shared their sack lunch out of habit.

"What are you talking about?" Bonnie responded.

"Because you work in the office, and I'm on the assembly line."

"I do not." Bonnie insisted. "Whatever gave you that idea?"

"You do." That's all Bubble would say. "You just do."

Weeks later, during a Friday night dinner with their families and parents at Bonnie's house, the arguments continued. "I just don't see how you can believe like you do," one of them remarked.

"I just believe the Bible—that's all."

"You believe *your interpretation* of the Bible. Your whole church is so off base. I could never believe like that."

"And I could never go to a church like yours. It's you that's wrong!"

The evening had ended early with both sisters in tears and the children and grandparents in puzzlement.

The weekly family visits grew further apart. And their conversations either skimmed the surface of life or ended in further hurt feelings. Over what, neither sister could exactly pinpoint after the air cleared.

Finally, one day while they each suffered in silence over Sunday lunch at their parents' house, Bubbles again broached a touchy subject.

Bonnie stopped her. "No, I don't want to hear another word. And I don't want to say another word. You're my sister, and I love you. And we're never going to argue about our religion—or anything—again. Ever!"

And they never have. Together, they've seen nineteen children and grandchildren baptized, and buried both parents and one husband. For the past thirty-eight years, they've been closer than when they first rolled down their socks at the bottom of the hill and around the curve.

∞ ∞ ∞

In the all-important world of family relations, three words are almost as powerful as the famous "I love you." They are "Maybe you're right."
—*Oren Arnold*

When one will not, two cannot quarrel.
—*Unknown*

Be kind and compassionate to one another, forgiving each other, just as in Christ God forgave you.
—*Ephesians 4:32*

 Words that Admire

I'VE BECOME MY MOTHER

Words can be a most special surprise gift:

To My Mom [Polly Haase Fuhrman]:

It is sometimes said, "Oh, no, I've become my mother!" My response to that comment? I hope to.

You are who I'd like to become. I admire your intelligence, your good judgment, your strength, and your beauty. I love you for your great warmth, sensitivity, generosity, and sense of humor.

Over the years, you've fulfilled many roles. At times you've been my guide, my teacher, my audience, my tutor, my confidante, my counselor, and my savior; but you've always been my best friend.

Thank you for always trusting me and believing in me. Thank you for always being someone I can trust and someone I can believe in.

Andrea

Is there someone you need to write today?

                     ✍ ✍ ✍

Words, when they're printed, have a life of their own.

—*Carol Burnett*

The Final Word

One odd note in preparing this book: A few of the people I asked about their high-impact conversations couldn't recall hearing *anything* of significance from the important women in their lives! Let's hope it's a memory failure rather than lack of influence from the wives, mothers, grandmothers, and friends in their lives.

If the words spoken to them have been negative, let's hope time has erased them. If the words spoken to them have been positive, let's hope time will deepen and endear them.

Nevertheless, our challenge as women remains to write or speak lasting legacies to those we love.

It's my hope that through this book we'll all realize the anguish caused by careless words and the power of positive words to change lives.

There are few greater responsibilities in life than to weigh our words with wisdom and kindness.

P.S. If this book has brought to your mind significant conversations from your own past, I invite you to forward your experiences to me for inclusion in my next book. (You can find my address in the For More Information section.) Thanks so much. And keep talking.

For More Information

ABOUT THE AUTHOR

*D*ianna Booher and her staff travel internationally, speaking and presenting seminars and training workshops on communication, motivational, and inspirational topics. A prolific author of more than thirty-six books, Dianna is CEO of Dallas-Ft. Worth-based Booher Consultants, a training firm specializing in communication skills. Her career as a professional speaker puts her in front of audiences ranging from churches to corporations. Her clients include IBM, Exxon, Hewlett Packard, Frito-Lay, MCI, Texas Instruments, Morgan Stanley Dean Witter, Salomon Smith Barney, and Deloitte & Touche, among others. She holds a master's degree from the University of Houston. She lives in the DFW metroplex with her husband, Vernon Rae.

If you would like more information regarding scheduling a workshop or a keynote, please contact:

Booher Consultants, Inc.
4001 Gateway Dr.
Colleyville, TX 76034-5917
Phone: 817-868-1200
E-mail: mailroom@booherconsultants.com
Web site: www.booherconsultants.com

OTHER RESOURCES BY DIANNA BOOHER

Books

The Little Book of Big Questions

Love Notes: From My Heart to Yours

Ten Smart Moves for Women Who Want to Succeed in Love and Life

Fresh-Cut Flowers for a Friend

First Thing Monday Morning

Get a Life Without Sacrificing Your Career: How to Find Time for the Really Important Things

Communicate with Confidence: How to Say It Right the First Time and Every Time

The Complete Letterwriter's Almanac

Clean Up Your Act: Effective Ways to Organize Paperwork and Get It Out of Your Life

Cutting Paperwork in the Corporate Culture

Executive's Portfolio of Model Speeches for All Occasions

Would You Put That in Writing?

Good Grief, Good Grammar

The New Secretary: How to Handle People As Well As You Handle Paper

Send Me a Memo: A Handbook of Model Memos

To the Letter: A Handbook of Model Letters for the Busy Executive

Great Personal Letters for Busy People

Writing for Technical Professionals

Winning Sales Letters

67 Presentation Secrets to Wow Any Audience

To-the-Point E-Mail and Voice Mail

Videotapes

Basic Steps for Better Business Writing (series)

Business Writing: Quick, Clear, Concise

Closing the Gap: Gender Communication Skills

Cutting Paperwork: Management Strategies

Cutting Paperwork: Support Staff Strategies

Audiotape Series

Get Your Book Publi$hed

People Power

Write to the Point: Business Communications from Memos to Meetings

Software (Disks and CD-ROM)

Effective Writing

Effective Editing

Good Grief, Good Grammar

More Good Grief, Good Grammar

Ready, Set, NeGOtiate

2001 Letters That Work

2001 Business Letters

2001 Sales and Marketing Letters

Model Personal Letters

8005 Model Quotes, Speeches, and Toasts

Workshops

Effective Writing

Technical Writing

To-the-Point E-Mail and Voice Mail

Developing Winning Proposals

Good Grief, Good Grammar

Customer Service Communications

Increasing Your Personal Productivity

Presentations That Work (oral presentations)

People Power (interpersonal skills)

People Productivity (interpersonal skills)

Listening Until You Really Hear

Resolving Conflict without Punching Someone Out

Leading and Participating in Productive Meetings

Negotiating So That Everyone Feels Like a Winner

Speeches

The Gender Communication Gap: "Did You Hear What I Think I Said?"

Communication: From Boardroom to Bedroom

Communication: The 10 Cs

Selling across Gender Lines

Communicating CARE to Customers

Write This Way to Success

Platform Tips for the Presenter

Get a Life Without Sacrificing Your Career

Putting Together the Puzzle of Personal Excellence

The Plan and the Purpose—Despite the Pain and the Pace

Ten Smart Moves for Women